Houghton Mifflin

TREASURE
LITERACY ACTIVITY BOOK

Senior Authors
J. David Cooper
John J. Pikulski

Authors
Kathryn H. Au
Margarita Calderón
Jacqueline C. Comas
Marjorie Y. Lipson
J. Sabrina Mims
Susan E. Page
Sheila W. Valencia
MaryEllen Vogt

Consultants
Dolores Malcolm
Tina Saldivar
Shane Templeton

INVITATIONS
TO LITERACY

Houghton Mifflin Company • Boston

Atlanta • Dallas • Geneva, Illinois • Palo Alto • Princeton

CONTENTS

CONTENTS

MAGIC PICTURES

Consonant Sounds and Letters

Bb bird

Cc cat

Dd dinosaur

Ff fish

Gg ghost

Hh horse

Jj jack-in-the-box

Kk king

Ll lion

Mm monster

Nn nurse

Pp pig

Qq queen

Rr rocket

Ss seal

Tt tiger

Vv vest

Ww worm

Xx x-ray

Yy yarn

Zz zebra

MAGIC PICTURES

Vowel Sounds and Letters

A a

alligator

acorn

E e

elephant

eel

I i
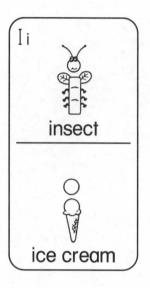
insect

ice cream

O o

ostrich

ocean

U u

umbrella

unicorn

Name

Let's Recycle It!

Help Harvey recycle. Cut out and paste the pictures
where they belong.

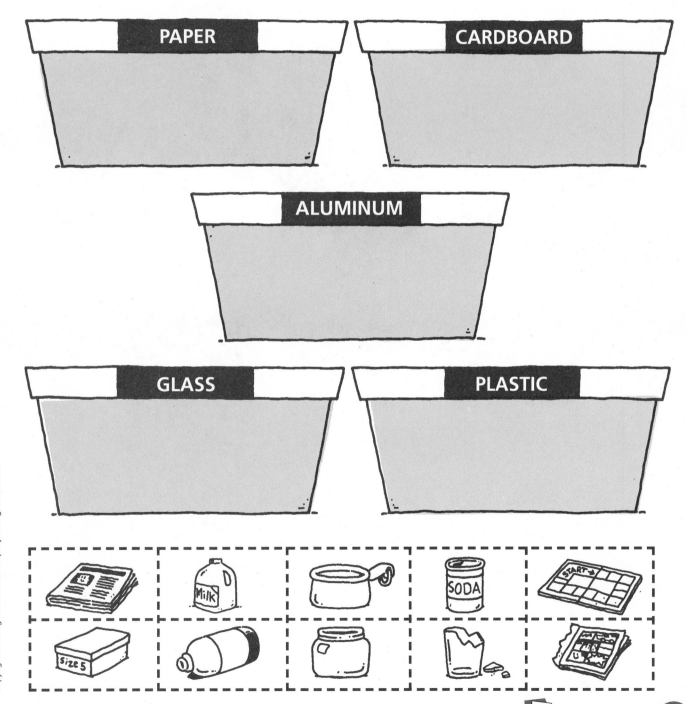

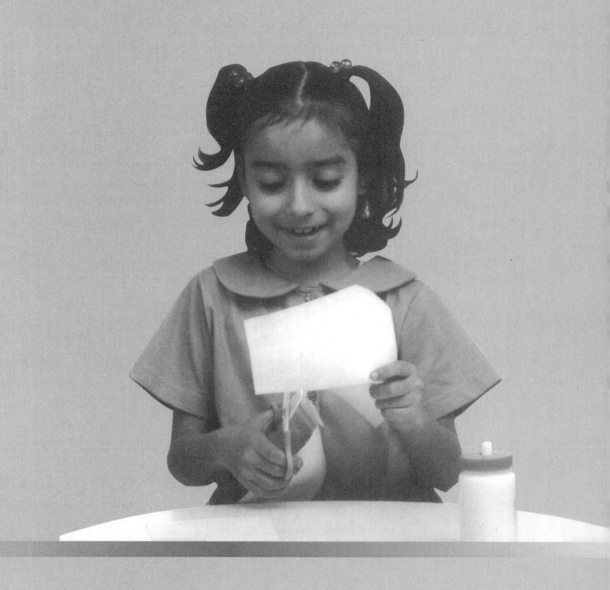

Name _____

Harvey Can Cook, Too

Finish the sentences with words from the box. Cut and paste the pictures that go with the sentences.

| cookies |
| broom |
| spoon |
| stool |
| newspaper |
| glued |

1 Harvey wants to

make _____.

2 Sometimes he finds recipes

in the _____.

3 His recipes are _____

into a cookbook.

4 Everything is stirred together with

a _____.

5 While the cookies bake, he waits on

a _____.

 Family Photos 5

Harvey's Garage Sale

Help Harvey write price tags for the things he wants to sell. Use these words.

clean

today

notice

few

shout

should

done

Don't _____ at your friends. Use this old phone to call them. $1

You _____ buy this ball _____. 25¢

Why not buy a _____ books? Then give them away when you are _____ with them. 12 for 50¢

Be sure to _____ how neat and _____ this used shirt is. $1

Family Photos 7

Make It Rhyme

Finish the poem about Harvey's cool cat. Write a sentence that rhymes with each line below.

Example:

Remember me? I'm Harvey's cool cat.
I'm striped and furry and a little bit fat.

1 I follow Harvey everywhere.

_____

2 Harvey needs me when he cleans his room.

_____

3 We work all day and don't even eat.

_____

4 We clean the closet and under the bed, too.

_____

5 And when at last we are all done,

_____

Name

Begin with a Brainstorm

Plan your poem.

List some topics. Circle the one you like best.

What do you want to tell about? Write your ideas.

What are some rhyming words you might use?

Family Photos **9**

Name _____

Harvey's Cleanup

Each Spelling Word is spelled with the
letters **oo**. These letters make two
different vowel sounds.

the 🌙 vowel sound → m**oo**n

the 📖 vowel sound → b**oo**k

Write the Spelling Words. Draw a line from each sock
to the drawer that has the matching vowel sound.

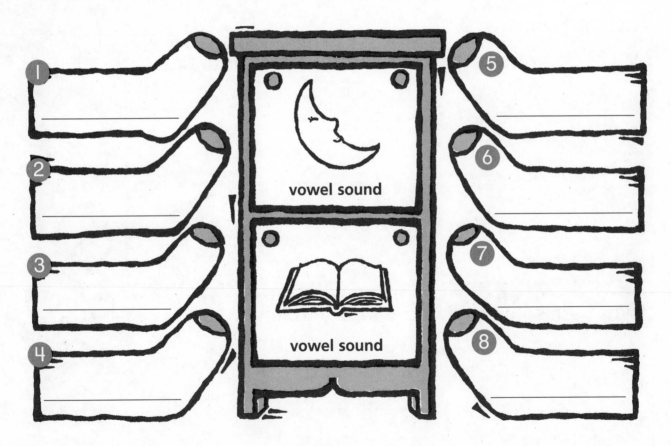

Which two Spelling Words rhyme with cook?

9 _____   10 _____

Name _____

Spelling Spree

Write a Spelling Word for each clue.

1. part of your leg ☐ __ __ __

2. to see with your eyes ☐ __ __ __

3. a place with four walls __ ☐ __ __

4. It shines at night. ☐ __ __ __

5. You clean with this. __ ☐ __ __ __

Where did Harvey put everything? Find out
by writing the letters in the boxes.

Secret Word: ☐ ☐ ☐ ☐ ☐

Find and circle three Spelling
Words that are spelled wrong in
this list. Then write each word
correctly.

6 _____

7 _____

8 _____

Things to Do Today

• Eat breakfast as sone as you get up.

• Pick up the clothes in your room.

• Sweep the floor with a broom.

• Return library bok.

• Eat lunch at nune.

Family Photos 11

Name ....

Working Words

What if Harvey had a robot to help him clean
his room! Finish each sentence to show what
Harvey tells his robot to do.

cook	sweep
wash	dust
walk	plant

"You will _____!"

"You will _____!"

"You will _____!"

"You will _____!"

"You will _____!"

"You will _____!"

Name

Tip the Piggy

Answer the question or follow the directions.

1 Jenny brought home some tips from her new job. Circle the tips.

2 Help Jenny count her money.

How many dollar bills? _____

How much change? _____

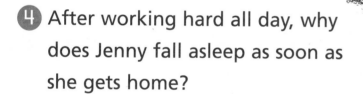

3 Jenny puts her savings in her piggy bank. Draw four dollars in the bank.

4 After working hard all day, why does Jenny fall asleep as soon as she gets home?

_____

5 When her bank gets full, Jenny wants to buy her mother the best present in the world. What do you think she will buy?

_____

6 What would you buy?

_____

_____

Name

Show and Tell

Write what each object is.

Tell what story event it makes you think about.

_____

_____

_____

_____

_____

_____

Name

What's Next?

Cut and paste the pictures to show what happens.
Then finish each story with your own sentence.

1 _____

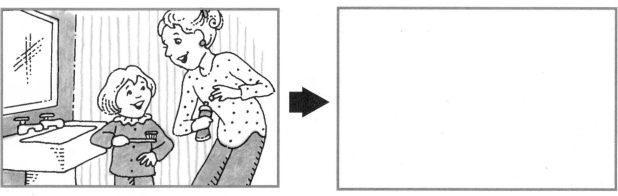

 2 _____

Family Photos **15**

Start a Scrapbook

Write the words that have the same vowel sound as the picture name.

arm	fall
far	first
girl	hard
shirt	small
start	wall
tall	third

1 _____

2 _____

3 _____

4 _____

5 _____

6 _____

7 _____

8 _____

9 _____

10 _____

11 _____

12 _____

Family Photos **17**

....

Name

Thanks a Bunch!

Use these words to complete each sentence. Then add today's date and finish the thank-you note.

brought	buy	fall	four	full	world

_____, 19_____

Dear Friends,

   My mother, my grandmother, and I want to thank you

for the food and furniture you _____

to our new apartment. You're my best friends in the

whole _____. The table and

_____ chairs look nice in our new kitchen.

Now, when our jar of money is _____,

we can _____ the big chair we are saving

for. I hope we get a big one, so I can sit beside Mama when

I _____ asleep.

_____

_____

_____

_____

_____

_____

_____

Name

Spend or Save?

Write the words from the box on the coins. Then
paste a word on each jar to make an opposite pair.

new	sad
day	left
last	open

1. close

2. right

3. happy

4. night

5. old

6. first

Write a sentence that uses the word pair from one jar.

_____

_____

Name

Journal Words

Write your ideas for your journal entry.

What do I want to write about?

Who was there? What did they say?

People	What They Said

What happened?

Events

Describing Words

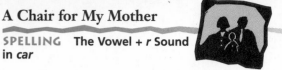

Name _____

Jars of Words

Each Spelling Word has a vowel sound that is
not short or long. It is the vowel sound that
you hear in **car**. This vowel sound is different
because the vowel is followed by **r**.

the vowel + **r** sound ➔ jar, arm

Write the missing Spelling Words to finish each clue.
Then draw a line under the letters that spell the
vowel + **r** sound.

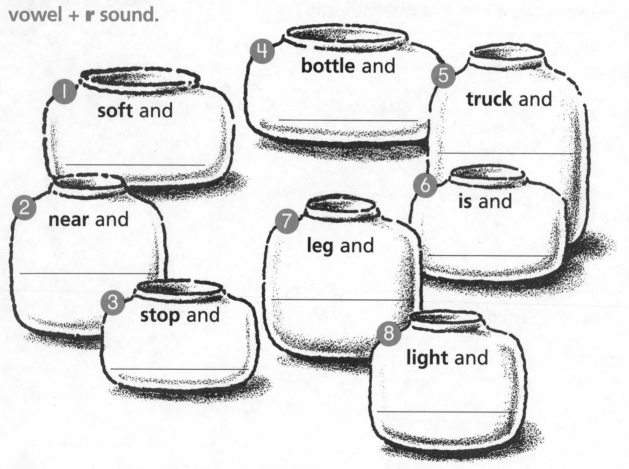

1. **soft** and _____

2. **near** and _____

3. **stop** and _____

4. **bottle** and _____

5. **truck** and _____

6. **is** and _____

7. **leg** and _____

8. **light** and _____

Which two Spelling Words begin with a vowel?

9 _____

10 _____

Spelling Spree

Write a Spelling Word to finish the
second sentence in each pair.

Spelling Words	
1. **jar**	5. **start**
2. **arm**	6. **car**
3. **hard**	7. **far**
4. **are**	8. **dark**

1. It is **light** outside during the **day**.
   It is ____ outside during the **night**.

2. A **pillow** is **soft**.
   A **rock** is ____.

3. Your **foot** is part of your **leg**.
   Your **hand** is part of your ____ .

4. A **bottle** has a **cap**.
   A ____ has a **lid**.

1 _____

2 _____

3 _____

4 _____

Find and circle four Spelling Words that are spelled
wrong in this ad. Then write each word correctly.

THE HOME STORE

Is your chair worn? Is the seat too hard? Buy a
new one! Our chairs ar the best in town. A big sale
will stard next week. The Home Store is not farr
from the airport. Park your kar in our big lot.

5 _____

6 _____

7 _____

8 _____

Name

Spare Change

Make sentences by choosing a coin from each jar.

Remember to add **s** to a verb that tells about one.

Write each sentence correctly.

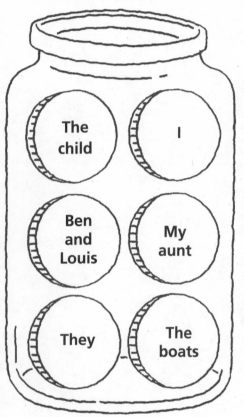

The child

I

Ben and Louis

My aunt

They

The boats

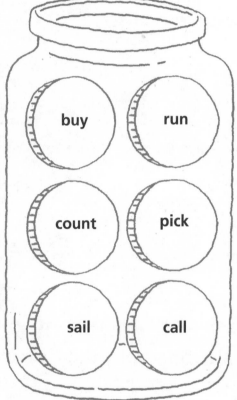

buy

run

count

pick

sail

call

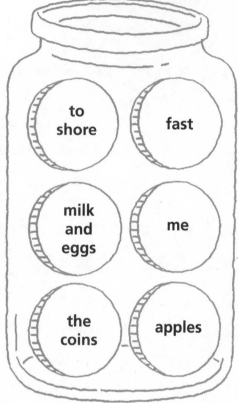

to shore

fast

milk and eggs

me

the coins

apples

 1 _____

 2 _____

 3 _____

 4 _____

 5 _____

6 _____

24 **Family Photos**

Plan It!

Draw pictures of what will happen in your story.

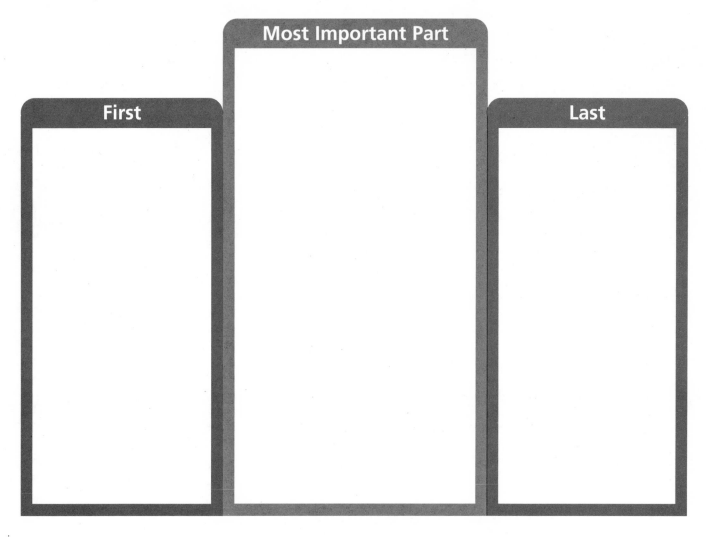

Most Important Part

First

Last

Write some sentences to tell about your pictures.

_____

_____

_____

_____

Name

Look Again

• Revising Checklist •

Answer these questions about your true story.

☐ Does my story keep to the topic?

☐ Have I told enough so the reader can picture what happens?

☐ Do I have a good beginning, middle, and end?

Questions to Ask My Writing Partner

• What do you like best about my true story?

• Is there anything that isn't clear?

• Is there anything I should add?

How I Can Make My Story Better

_____

_____

_____

_____

_____

Name

Step By Step

Finish this puzzle. Use the word that fits each clue.

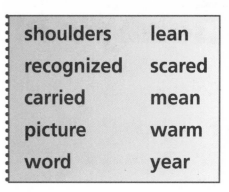

shoulders	lean
recognized	scared
carried	mean
picture	warm
word	year

Down

1. parts of the body
2. afraid
3. to rest on something
4. something you take with a camera
7. a group of letters
8. "I didn't ____ to do it!"

Across

5. held something and took it somewhere
6. knew who someone was
7. not cool
9. twelve months

Name

Bobby's Photo Album

Complete each sentence in the album. Draw a
picture to go with each sentence.

When Bobby was a baby,

_____

_____

_____

When Bobby was

growing up, _____

_____

_____

On Bobby's fifth birthday,

_____

_____

_____

When Bob went to the

hospital, _____

_____

_____

Name

Bobby's Diary

Cut out and paste the notes in Bobby's diary in the order that they happened.

Bob came home today.

Bob walked to the end of the lawn.

Bob smiled a little when I made a tower with blocks.

Bob doesn't remember me.

Bob leaned on me and started to walk.

 Family Photos **29**

Find the Hidden Word

Write a word from the box to fit each clue.

core	shore
torn	corn
sport	worn

1 ripped ⬜ __ __ __

2 eat it on the cob __ ⬜ __ __

3 what was done with a shirt ⬜ __ __ __

4 center of an apple __ __ __ ⬜

5 land next to a lake __ __ __ ⬜ __

6 game such as baseball ⬜ __ __ __ __

Now write the letters from the boxes to
make a word that finishes the sentence.

7 Bob and Bobby made 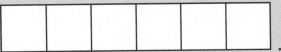 .

Name _____

Sign Makers

Help get the amusement park ready for Bob
and Bobby's visit. Write a word from a
balloon to finish each sign.

carried

warm

year

picture

mean

word

1 Get your

_____

taken here!

2 HOT FOOD

Are you cold? You can

_____ up here.

3 DARTS

ball
fish
bear
ring
bear
fish
ball

Hit the

_____

and win a prize.

4 ROCKET RIDE

This rocket ship is just
like the one that

_____

the first people to the moon.

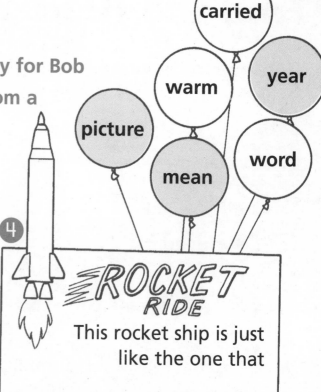

5 MONSTER
ROLLER COASTER

We don't _____
to scare you, but it is
a long way down!

6 I will guess the

_____

you were born.

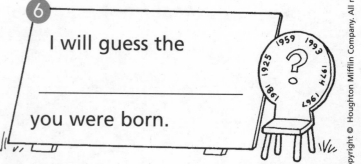

Name _____

How Many Syllables?

How many parts does each word have? Write the
word next to the block that tells the number of parts.

| better | hospital | talk | monster | sneeze |
| tower | spoon | shoulders | slowly | grandfather |

1 _____   _____ **1**

2 _____   _____ **1**

2 _____   _____ **2**

2 _____   _____ **2**

3 _____   _____ **3**

Use two words from the box in a sentence of your own. Circle all
the words with one syllable and underline all the words with two.

_____

_____

Name

Together Again

Write about a special day for Bob and
Bobby. Use verbs from the box.
Draw a picture to show what happens.

grabbed
shouted
glided
danced
gulped
romped
studied
tiptoed

Name

Step by Step

Each Spelling Word has the vowel + **r**
sound that you hear in **store**. This sound
is often spelled **or** or **ore**.

the vowel + r sound ➔ for, more

l. **for**	5. **born**
2. **more**	6. **short**
3. **or**	7. **store**
4. **story**	8. **corn**

Your Own Words

Write the Spelling Words. Color orange each word in
which the vowel + **r** sound is spelled **or**. Color yellow
each word in which the vowel + **r** sound is spelled **ore**.

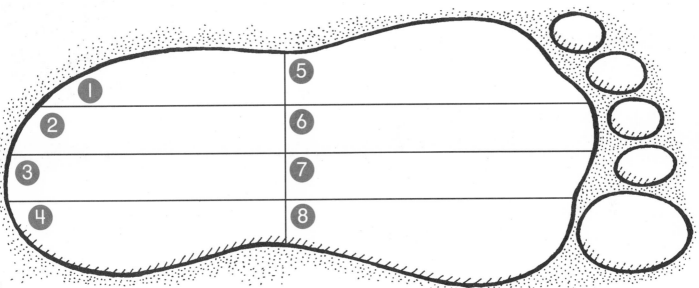

Write Spelling Words to answer the questions.

9 Which word begins with the **sh** sound? _____

10 Which word begins and ends like **barn**? _____

Name _____

Spelling Spree

Write the Spelling Word that matches
each clue.

1 a shop _____

2 a newly ____ baby _____

3 a vegetable _____

4 a tale _____

5 tall or ____ _____

Find and circle three Spelling Words that are spelled wrong
in these get-well cards. Then write each word correctly.

I miss you mor

every day.

Get better so

we can play.

This short poem

is just fer you.

Get well soon

orr I will be blue.

6 _____

7 _____

8 _____

All in the Past

Use the clues to write a verb that tells about the past. Use the words in the box to help you.

talk	miss
jump	look
trick	brush
play	walk

1. cleaned the teeth
   __ __ __ __ □ __ __

2. watched
   __ □ __ __ __

3. didn't catch the bus
   __ __ __ □ __

4. leaped
   __ __ __ □ __

5. fooled someone
   __ __ □ __ __ __

6. spoke
   □ __ __ __ __

7. had fun
   __ __ □ __ __

8. went by foot
   __ □ __ __ __

Answer the question by writing the boxed letters.

Where did Bob go when he was sick?

□ □ □ □ □ □ □ □

Family Photos 37

Name

The Ring's the Thing

Follow the rhyme trail and complete the rhymes.

| nearly shock second light confess |

1

My ring looked white

In the bright _____.

2

Had I put it there?
I couldn't find it anywhere.

3

It was a _____
Not to find it by the clock.

4

Where could a ring hide?

I _____ cried.

5

Had someone, somewhere
Swallowed my ring?

6

Wait a _____,
Who would do such a thing?

7

I had to _____
This was such a mess.

8

"Let me interrupt you," Mother said.
"Look what is here by the book
    that I read."

9

I had to laugh. I began to sing.
After all, I did not lose the ring!

Name

Tamale Test!

Circle **True** or **Not True**.

1. Maria made tamales by herself.   True   Not True

2. Maria was unhappy about making tamales.   True   Not True

3. Maria wanted to try on the diamond ring.   True   Not True

4. Maria's mother never took off the ring.   True   Not True

5. Maria was worried when the ring was missing.   True   Not True

6. Maria thought the ring fell into the trash.   True   Not True

7. Maria and her cousins ate all the tamales.   True   Not True

8. They found the ring in the last tamale.   True   Not True

9. Maria's mother was angry that Maria had
   played with her diamond ring.   True   Not True

10. Maria's whole family made a second batch
    of tamales.   True   Not True

Choose two sentences that are
not true. On the back of this
paper, rewrite each sentence
to make it true.

Family Photos 39

Rewrite two sentences to make them true.

_____

_____

_____

_____

_____

_____

Story Chain

Write a story part in each box. Make a
chain by gluing the boxes in order. Write
your name in the title box.

```
TOO MANY TAMALES
Retold by: _____
```

Glue here | **Setting:**

Glue here | **Event:**

Glue here | **Main Characters:**

Glue here | **Event:**

Glue here | **Problem:**

Glue here | **Event:**

Glue here | **Event:**

Glue here | **Ending:**

Use the story chain to retell the story to a partner.

Name

Tips for Tamales

Write a word beginning on each line to complete the
word that best fits the tip.

| Word Beginnings |
| re   dis   un |

1. You will need to _____heat the tamale if it cools

   a little.

2. If you are _____able to take off the corn husk,

   ask for help.

3. You can save the husks and _____use them the

   next time you make tamales.

4. Don't _____wrap the filling.

5. If you _____like the taste at first, don't give up

   on this special food.

Write your own tamale tip using a word with **re**, **dis**,
or **un**.

_____

_____

....

Name

Maria's Family Album

Write a word to complete each sentence. Then draw
a line between the base word and ending of the
word you wrote.

| taller | opened | fastest | laughed | drinking |

1. Teresa is _____ milk.

2. Maria is the _____ runner.

3. Maria is _____ than Teresa.

4. Teresa _____ a gift.

5. We _____ at the funny story.

Name

A Recipe for Fun

Cut out the words at the bottom of the page.
Paste the words in the boxes to
finish the recipe.

Toast Treats

1 Pour a little milk into four glasses. Use [ ] milk, not chocolate or strawberry.

2 Add a few drops of food coloring to each glass. In the first glass, add red. In the [ ] glass, add blue. In the third, add yellow. In the last, add green.

3 Put the bread in the toaster until it is [ ] brown, not dark brown.

4 Paint a picture on the toast with the colored milk.

5 Toast the bread again. Have a grown-up check the toast when you think it's [ ] done. The picture won't show if the toast gets burned.

6 Does the picture make you smile or [ ]? Make a Toast Treat for someone else and make them happy, too!

Now cut out the recipe card. You might try this recipe at home.

| second | laugh | white | light | nearly |

Name

Helpful Cooks

Everyone can help make tamales. Write
a sentence for each picture. Use a word
from the box in each sentence.

armful	cupful
handful	mouthful

① _____

_____

_____

③ _____

_____

_____

② _____

_____

_____

④ _____

_____

_____

 Family Photos 47

Name

Let's Eat Out

Look at the picture. Write complete sentences about
what is happening. You might use words from the box.

| laughing | throwing | eating | talking | happy |
| hungry | family | baby | father | boy |

_____

_____

_____

_____

_____

_____

_____

Name _____

Crossword House

Each Spelling Word has the vowel + **r**
sound that you hear at the end of 🌸.
This sound is often spelled **er**.

the vowel + r sound → bett**er**, aft**er**

Write a Spelling Word for each clue
in the puzzle. Then color the squares
that have the letters that spell
the vowel + **r** sound.

Across

3. a woman in
    a family

4. a girl in a family

5. a man in a family

7. good, ____, best

8. below

Down

1. a boy in a family

2. above

6. before and ____

Spelling Words

1. **better**   5. **mother**
2. **after**   6. **father**
3. **over**   7. **sister**
4. **under**   8. **brother**

✏️ Your Own Words

Write Spelling Words to answer the questions.

9. Which word begins like **monster**? _____

10. Which word begins like **seed**? _____

Spelling Spree

Write a Spelling Word to name each
person in this family tree.

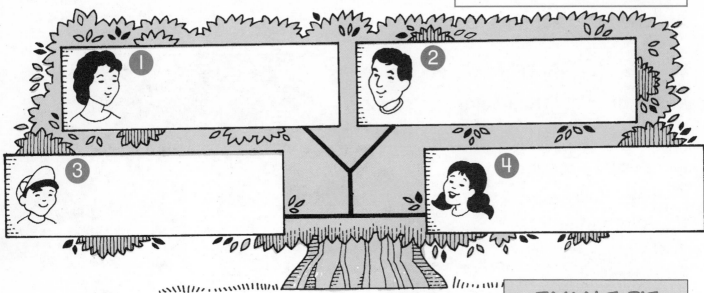

Find and circle four Spelling
Words that are spelled wrong in
this recipe. Then write each
word correctly.

5 _____

6 _____

7 _____

8 _____

TAMALE PIE

Follow these steps to make a
tamale pie.

◆ Add 1 cup of cornmeal to
4 cups of water and cook for
45 minutes.

◆ Spread the mix in a pan aftur
you grease it.

◆ Spread tomatoes and meat ovr
the mix. Red tomatoes are
beter than green ones.

◆ Brown the tamales undar the
broiler.

Have your mother or father try
this tasty dish!

To Be or Not to Be

Write sentences to answer the questions
about the picture.

1 Who is very hungry?

_____

2 Where were the vegetables?

_____

3 How many places are there at the table?

_____

4 Where was the puppy?

_____

Write your own sentence about the picture.
Use **is**, **are**, **was**, or **were**.

_____

_____

Name

Late Again!

Mia has a big problem. She needs her family's help to solve it. So Mia taped this note to the kitchen cupboard.

Dear Family,

    I was late to school again today! I fell back asleep after Mom woke me up. Then I got dressed in a hurry, but my socks didn't match. Uncle Joe made me change them. Next, Grandma gave me a huge bowl of oatmeal. She made me eat all of it. Then I had to wait for Frank to get out of the bathroom. I ran to school. But I was still late, and my teacher was upset.

    Please think of a way to help me be on time tomorrow!

Love,
Mia

Make a Story Cartoon

Make a story cartoon that tells what Mia's family will do tomorrow to help Mia get to school on time. Use a separate sheet of paper to write down your ideas in story order.

Cartoon Checklist

- ☐ My pictures show how Mia's family helped her.
- ☐ I have drawn my pictures in story order.
- ☐ I can explain my cartoon clearly to others.

Name

Tales and Details

Read the ad about a lost boa constrictor and complete the chart.

MISSING

Please help me find my boa constrictor! It is brown with
large and small tan spots. It is 12 feet long and likes to
meet animals. It was last seen on a farm with a large load
of wash. It was crawling through a pair of blue jeans and
swallowing a white shirt.

Details About the Boa

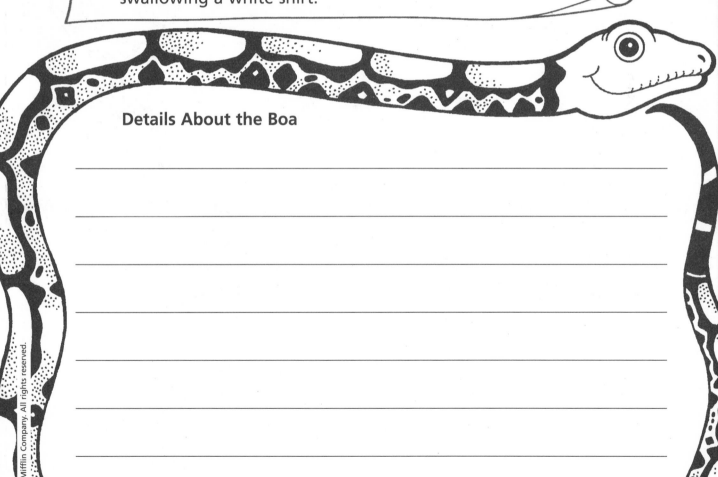

_____

_____

_____

_____

_____

_____

_____

That's Incredible! 53

Name

Bye-Bye, Boa

Read each sentence and look at the picture. Choose the
word that goes with the sentence and write it on the line.
Then underline the base word in the word you wrote.

| running | spotted | mopping | lunches | pigs |

1 A minute ago, the farmer

_____

the snake in the hen house.

2 The farmer is _____
to the hen house.

3 Now he is _____
up the mess in the hen house.

4 Meanwhile, the _____
are in the school bus.

5 They are eating all the children's

_____.

54 That's Incredible!

Coming Soon

Use words from the box to complete the movie ad. Then draw a picture showing your favorite scene from the movie.

class	farm
finally	sound
egg	hurry

THE DAY JIMMY'S BOA ATE THE WASH

The movie you've waited for is

_____

at a theater near you!

Mrs. Stanley's second-grade

_____

has a day they will never forget. It all begins with a simple trip to a

_____ .

If that doesn't _____ exciting, just wait!
You won't believe what happens when a hen lays an

_____ .

What does all this have to do with a boa that ate the wash? If you

want to find out, _____ to the theater.
You'll be glad you did!

Name

Sounds Alike

Follow the directions to complete the picture.

1 Draw two **pairs** of **pears** in the tree.

2 Next **to** the flower, draw **two** bees.

3 Look **for** the kittens. Draw **four** bowls
of milk near them.

4 Circle the chipmunk's **hole**. Color the
whole watermelon green.

Write a sentence about the picture.

Use one or more of the words in dark type.

_____

_____

One Thing After Another

Fix Jimmy's letter. Cross out the underlined words.
Write **He**, **She**, **It**, or **They** above the words you
crossed out.

Dear Rick,

My class went to a farm. I brought my boa along.

My boa got away! My boa went into the hen house. The hens

went wild. The hens flew all over. The farmer tried to catch

them. The farmer did not have much luck.

Then a chicken dropped an egg on Jenny's head. Jenny was

very mad. Jenny threw an egg at Tommy. Tommy ducked. The

egg hit Marianne! The egg dripped all over her hair. Her hair

was a mess!

The farmer and his wife were mad. The farmer and his wife

may never ask us back.

Your friend,

Jimmy

That's Incredible! 57

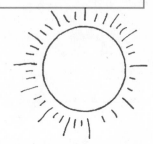

Name

Laundry for Lunch

Each Spelling Word names more than one
of something. The **s** and **es** endings
make these words mean more than one.

Add **s** to most words to name more than
one. Add **es** to words that end with **s**, **x**,
sh, or **ch** to name more than one.

s → trip**s**, egg**s**
es → bus**es**, box**es**, wish**es**, pea**ch**es

Spelling Words	
1. **trips**	5. **wishes**
2. **buses**	6. **boxes**
3. **classes**	7. **games**
4. **eggs**	8. **peaches**

 Your Own Words

Add **s** or **es** to the words hanging from the clothesline
to make Spelling Words. Write the words you made.

s   **es**

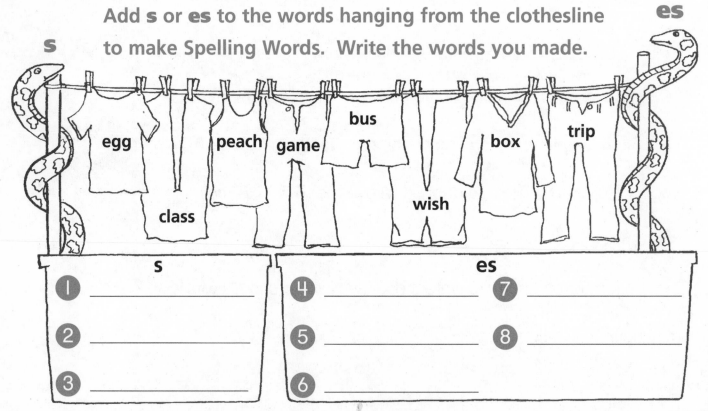

egg   class   peach   game   bus   wish   box   trip

s

1. _____
2. _____
3. _____

es

4. _____   7. _____
5. _____   8. _____
6. _____

Which two Spelling Words begin with a consonant cluster?

9. _____   10. _____

Name _____

Spelling Spree

Think how the words in each group are
alike. Write the missing Spelling Words.

1. cars, trucks, _____

2. apples, pears, _____

3. milk, butter, _____

4. crate, cartons, _____

Spelling Words	
1. **trips**	5. **wishes**
2. **buses**	6. **boxes**
3. **classes**	7. **games**
4. **eggs**	8. **peaches**

① _____

② _____

③ _____

④ _____

Find and circle four Spelling Words that are spelled wrong
in this notice. Then write each word correctly.

To: All Students _____

From: The Principal _____

    Your wishiz have come true!
On Friday, we will take the first of
many field tripps this year. All
klasses will meet in front of the
school. You may play gaims on the
buses, but please do not stand up.

⑤ _____

⑥ _____

⑦ _____

⑧ _____

Name _____

Those Are the Breaks!

Jenny and Sid are remembering their trip to the farm, but they don't know which verbs to use. Write the verbs that tell about the past. Then write an ending for the story. Use a verb that tells about the past.

Jenny: The trip to the farm last week was so much fun!

I (throw, threw) _____ an egg at the side of the barn.

Sid: You did? What happened?

Jenny: It (break, broke) _____ and made an awful

mess. Don't you remember?

Sid: No, I (take, took) _____ a nap on the bus.

The trip (make, made) _____ me sleepy. What

happened next?

Jenny: The teacher (make, made) _____ me

clean it up.

_____

_____

_____

Name

What's Up, Dinosaur?

Finish each sentence by writing the correct word from the box. Then cut out the pieces and put them together.

cold
leave
bored
often
guess
invented
later

I _____ think about dinosaurs.

The earth may have become too _____ for the dinosaurs.

Scientists _____ ways to tell how old dinosaur bones are.

Once there were many of them, but _____ there were none.

what made dinosaurs extinct.

I can _____

I read about dinosaurs.

Whenever I am

Why did the dinosaurs _____ the earth?

Name

A Dinosaur's Tale

Imagine you are a dinosaur visiting Earth.
You are on a talk show. Answer the questions.

How did you get along with people on Earth?

1 _____

_____

How did people get cars, houses, and airplanes?

2 _____

_____

If you did all those things for people, what did people do?

3 _____

_____

Why did you leave Earth? How did you leave?

4 _____

_____

What else would you like to tell?

_____

_____

Name

Really? Not Really!

Write **real** if the picture shows something that could happen in real life. Write **fantasy** if the picture shows something that could happen only in a fantasy story.

_____

_____

_____

_____

Write a sentence about something that could happen in real life.

_____

_____

Write a sentence about something that could happen only in a fantasy story.

_____

_____

64 That's Incredible!

Name

Scrambled Eggs

Cut and paste the eggs onto the nests to complete the sentences.
Be sure that the completed sentences make sense and
that they rhyme.

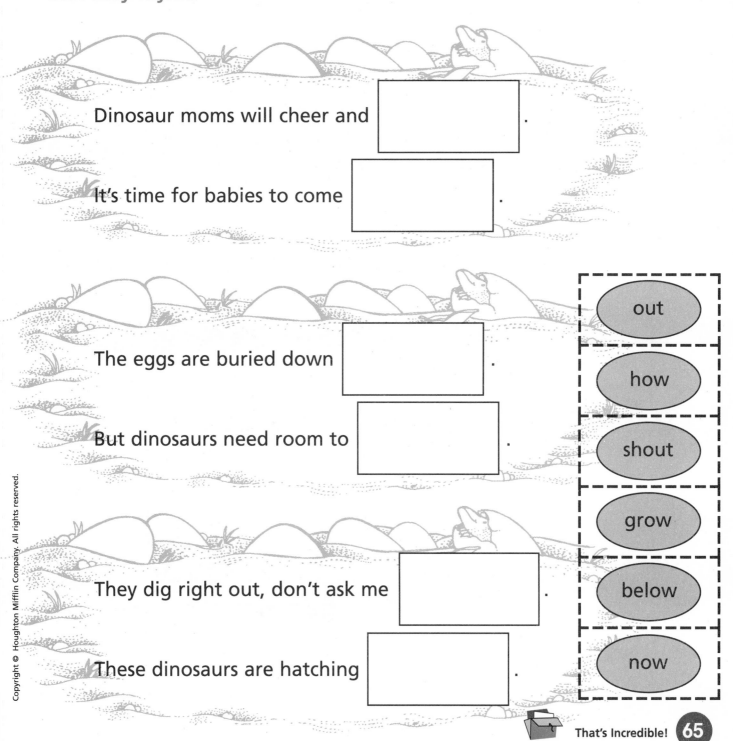

Dinosaur moms will cheer and

It's time for babies to come

The eggs are buried down

But dinosaurs need room to

They dig right out, don't ask me

These dinosaurs are hatching

out

how

shout

grow

below

now

That's Incredible! **65**

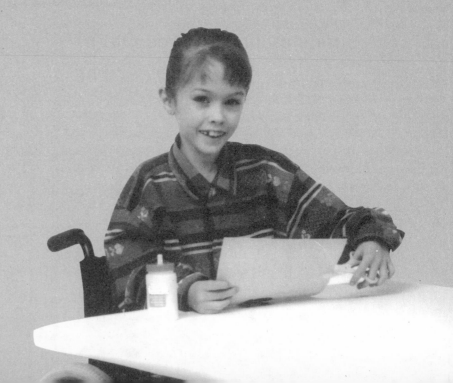

Dinosaur Bones

Write each word next to its definition.

| cold | guess | later | leave | often |

1 Many times. _____

2 Not warm or hot. _____

3 A time after now. _____

4 To try to think of an answer.

_____

5 To go away from a place.

_____

Write sentences about dinosaurs, using at least three words that you wrote.

_____

_____

_____

_____

Name

A Dinosaur's Circus

Look at the picture. Use a word in the box plus **'s** to complete each sentence. The first one has been done for you.

| boy |
| dinosaur |
| girl |
| bicycle |
| clown |

Example:

Look! There is a boy riding on a <u>dinosaur's</u> tail!

1 The _____ hat is as tall as the roof.

2 That _____ costume matches the dinosaur.

3 The _____ shoes are big and silly.

4 The _____ wheel is bigger than the dinosaur riding it.

Write two sentences about the scene. Use some words with **'s**.

5 _____

_____

6 _____

_____

Name

Here's Why!

Imagine that a dinosaur showed up in your back yard. Write some reasons to persuade your family to let you keep it.

Reason 1

Reason 2

Reason 3

That's Incredible! **69**

Name ....

Dino Doings

Each Spelling Word has the vowel sound that you hear in . This vowel sound may be spelled **ow** or **ou**.

the  vowel sound → how, out

Write the missing letters to make Spelling Words.
Then write the words under the matching spelling
for the vowel sound in  .

```
        m
     c  _  _
  h  _  s  e
        e
b r _  _  n
   d  _  n
      t
```

ou

1 _____

2 _____

3 _____

ow

4 _____

5 _____

6 _____

7 _____

8 _____

Which two Spelling Words begin like ?

9 _____   10 _____

Spelling Spree

Each missing letter fits in ABC order between the other letters. Write the missing letters. Then use the missing letters to write the Spelling Words.

Spelling Words	
I. **how**	5. **down**
2. **out**	6. **brown**
3. **now**	7. **cow**
4. **house**	8. **mouse**

Example: n __o__ p   t __u__ v   s __t__ u   **out**

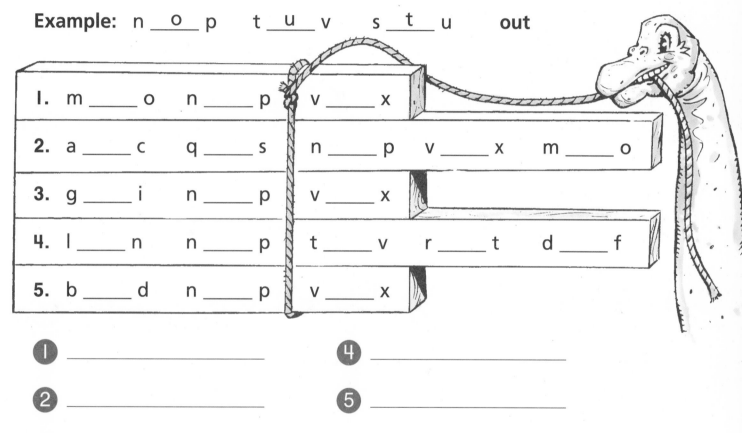

I. m ____ o   n ____ p   v ____ x

2. a ____ c   q ____ s   n ____ p   v ____ x   m ____ o

3. g ____ i   n ____ p   v ____ x

4. l ____ n   n ____ p   t ____ v   r ____ t   d ____ f

5. b ____ d   n ____ p   v ____ x

1. _____   4. _____

2. _____   5. _____

3. _____

Find and circle three Spelling Words that are spelled wrong on these signs. Then write each word correctly.

6. New Hous Now Being Built

7. Slow Doun! Workers Ahead

8. Watch Owt! Dinosaurs At Work

6. _____

7. _____

8. _____

....

Name

Riddle Time

Write the contraction that is the opposite of the word in **dark print** to finish each riddle. Then answer each riddle.

1 Sharks **did**, but most dinosaurs

_____.

_____

2 A frog **can**, but a dog

_____.

_____

3 A bird **does**, but a cat

_____.

_____

4 My parrot **could**, but my gerbil

_____.

_____

5 Monkeys **can**, but whales

_____.

_____

Now write your own riddle.

_____

_____

Putting It Together

Cut out the definition puzzle pieces. Match each definition
to the correct word. Paste the puzzle piece in the space.

What does the picture show? _____

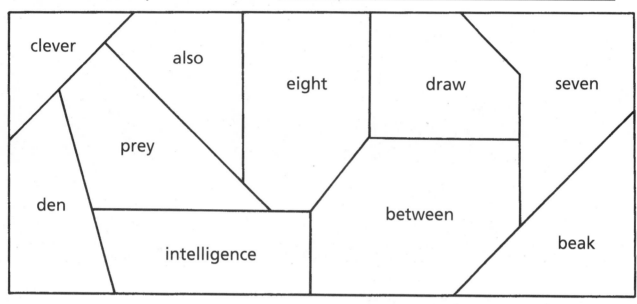

clever

also

eight

draw

seven

prey

den

between

intelligence

beak

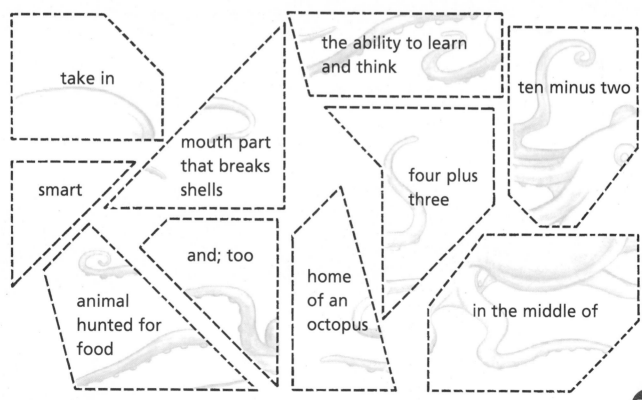

take in

the ability to learn
and think

ten minus two

smart

mouth part
that breaks
shells

four plus
three

and; too

animal
hunted for
food

home
of an
octopus

in the middle of

Name

It's Amazing!

Write words in the blanks to finish the newspaper article.

New Facts About the _____

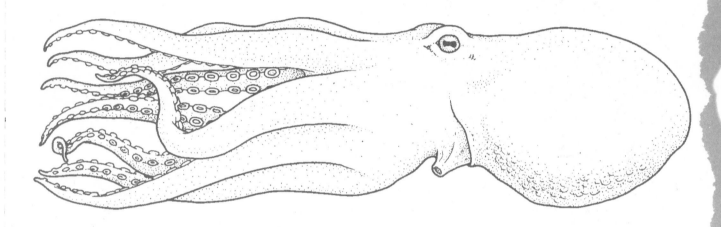

People have found out many facts about the octopus. Every octopus lives _____ in a den. An octopus can change _____ to match its surroundings. It can catch and hold food with the _____ on its arms.

An octopus can jet through the sea by drawing in _____ and shooting it out through its siphon. If an enemy tears off an octopus's arm, the arm _____. A female octopus weaves strings of _____ and hangs them in her den.

Octopuses also show signs of _____ by being able to solve problems. Really, an octopus is amazing!

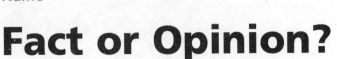

Name

Fact or Opinion?

Write **Fact** if the sentence can be proved. Write **Opinion**
if the sentence tells what someone feels or believes.

1 An octopus spends its life alone. _____

2 It would be very lonely to be an octopus. _____

3 An octopus has no backbone. _____

4 I believe that the blue-ringed octopus is the most beautiful

octopus of all. _____

5 I don't think I would ever like to see an octopus swimming next

to me. _____

6 An octopus eats crabs and lobsters. _____

Now write one fact and one opinion about an octopus.

7 Fact: _____

_____

_____

8 Opinion: _____

_____

_____

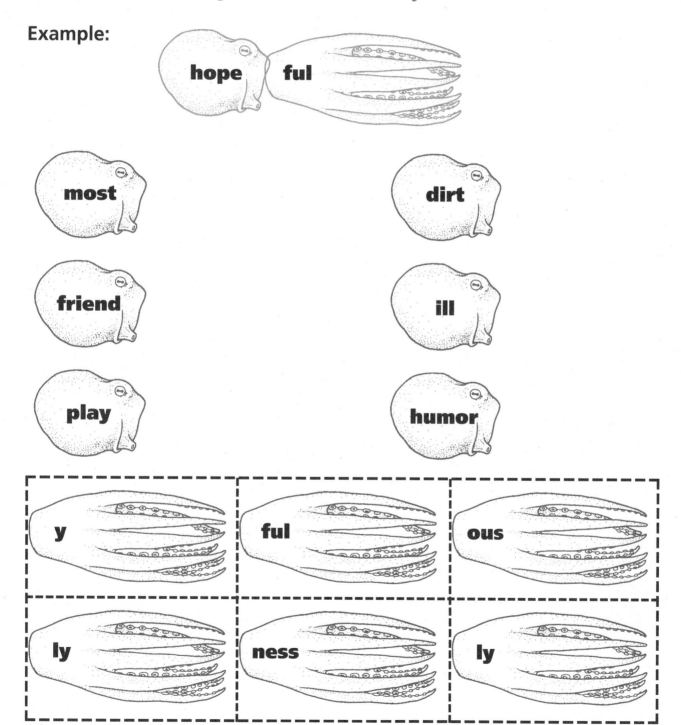

Attach the Tentacles

Cut and paste endings to make words. On the back of this paper, write sentences using three of the words you made.

Example:

hope ful

most

dirt

friend

ill

play

humor

y

ful

ous

ly

ness

ly

Write sentences using three of the words you made.

1. _____

_____

2. _____

_____

3. _____

_____

The Amazing Octopus

Write the words that make sense in the sentences.

almost	small	crawl	drawing

1 An octopus was born. It was very _____.

2 For a month, the baby octopus could not swim

or _____.

3 The octopus learned to swim by _____

in water and squirting it out.

4 Soon it was _____ strong enough to open a

clam.

Write four sentences of your own about an octopus.
Use one word from the box in each sentence.

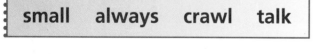

draw	raw	also	saw
small	always	crawl	talk

5 _____

6 _____

7 _____

8 _____

Name _____

Label the Diagram

Read the words in the box. Use the words to complete the labels on the diagram.

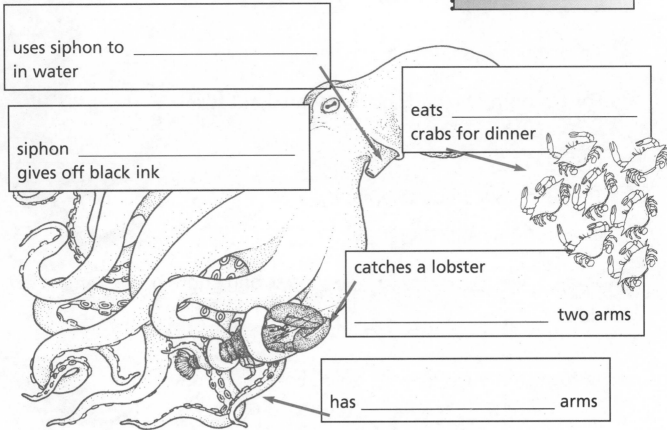

uses siphon to _____ in water

siphon _____ gives off black ink

eats _____ crabs for dinner

catches a lobster

_____ two arms

has _____ arms

Write a few sentences about the diagram. Use some words from the box.

_____

_____

_____

_____

_____

Find the Meanings

Read the words and their definitions. Then decide which definition fits each sentence. Write the correct definition.

leaves	1. Goes away from.	**store**	1. A place to buy things.
	2. Parts of a plant.		2. To keep for later use.
show	1. A performance.		
	2. To demonstrate.		

① An octopus **leaves** its den to hunt for food.

_____

② The **leaves** on the tree are green.

_____

③ An octopus can **show** how it feels by changing color.

_____

④ The seals put on a great **show** at the aquarium.

_____

⑤ Sometimes octopuses **store** crabs in their suckers to eat later.

_____

⑥ Did you buy anything at the fish **store**?

_____

On a separate sheet of paper, draw a picture showing one of the meanings of **leaves**, **show**, or **store**. See if a partner can guess which meaning you drew.

That's Incredible! **81**

Name

What I See

Imagine you are a scientist visiting an aquarium. You are watching an octopus and some other sea creatures. Write about what you see first, next, and last.

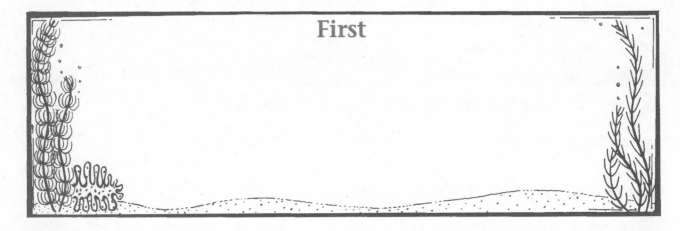

First

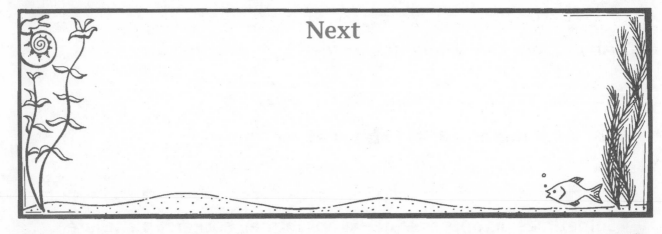

Next

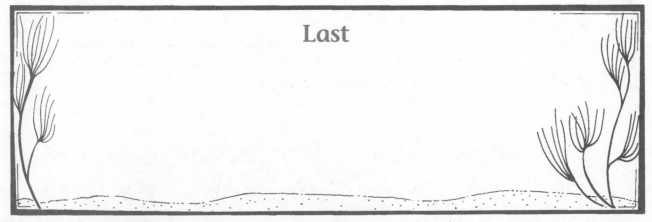

Last

Name

Simply Amazing

Each Spelling Word has the vowel sound that you hear in . This vowel sound may be spelled **aw** or **a** before **ll**.

the 🐚 vowel sound ➡ dr**aw**, **all**

Spelling Words	
1. **all**	5. **small**
2. **call**	6. **ball**
3. **draw**	7. **fall**
4. **saw**	8. **paw**

✏ Your Own Words

Write the missing letters to make Spelling Words.
Then write the words on the rock that has the
matching spelling for the vowel sound in 🐚.

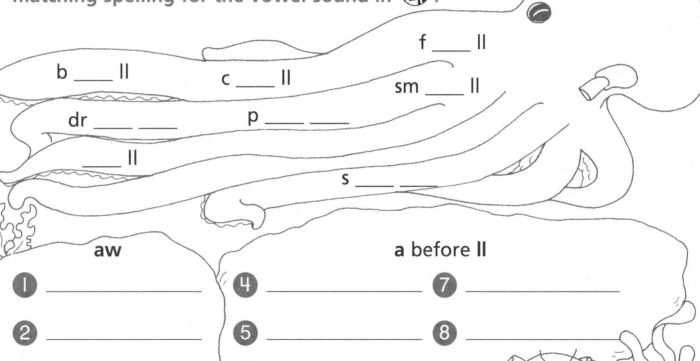

f ____ ll

b ____ ll   c ____ ll   sm ____ ll

dr ____ ____   p ____ ____

____ ll

s ____ ____

aw

1 _____
2 _____
3 _____

a before **ll**

4 _____
5 _____
6 _____

7 _____
8 _____

Write Spelling Words to answer the questions.

9 Which word begins like **pet**? _____

10 Which word begins like **dress**? _____

That's Incredible!   83

Name

Spelling Spree

Spelling Words	
1. **all**	5. **small**
2. **call**	6. **ball**
3. **draw**	7. **fall**
4. **saw**	8. **paw**

Write the word that goes with each clue.

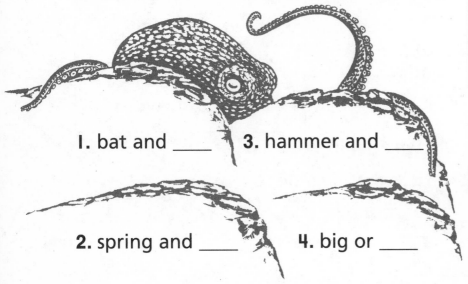

1. bat and ____   **3.** hammer and ___

2. spring and ___   **4.** big or ___

1 _____

2 _____

3 _____

4 _____

Find and circle four Spelling Words that are spelled wrong in this news story. Then write each word correctly.

Class News

My Diving Trip

On Tuesday my mother got a cal from my uncle. He asked us awl to go diving. We had a good time. I saw a baby octopus. It was only the size of a cat's pau. My uncle asked me to drow a picture of it. Here it is.

5 _____

6 _____

7 _____

8 _____

Name

The Sea Around Us

Find the picture that each sentence tells about. Then write the verb from that picture to complete the sentence correctly.

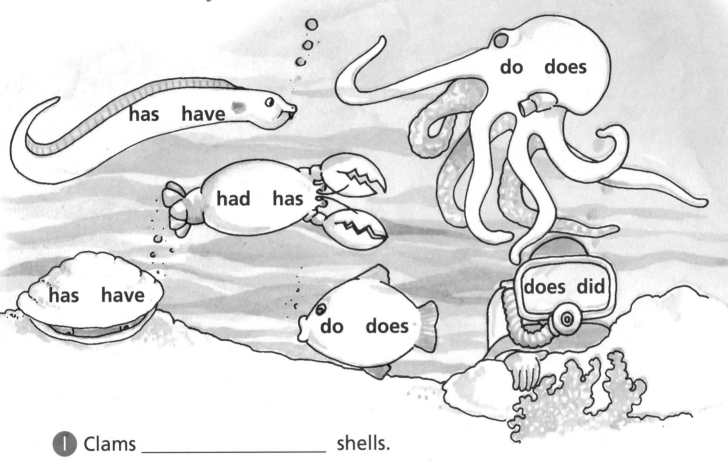

1 Clams _____ shells.

2 A moray eel _____ sharp teeth.

3 Yesterday the lobster _____ a good meal.

4 An octopus _____ amazing things.

5 Some fish _____ well in tanks.

6 Last week the diver _____ a practice dive.

Name _____

K-W-L Chart

Write what you know about your topic. Next, write what you want to know.
Then write what you have learned.

What I **K**now	What I **W**ant to Know	What I Have **L**earned

Revising

• Revising Checklist •

Write your answers to these questions.

Did I check to make sure I wrote

my facts correctly? _____

Are there any facts I would like to add?

_____

_____

Questions to Ask My Writing Partner

• What do you like best about my report?

• Is there anything you didn't understand?

• Have I told enough facts?

• What else would you like to know?

Making a Comic Book

Make your own incredible comic book.

First, think of a story that is amazing but true—or mostly true.

My comic book will be about:

_____

_____

Use frames, or boxes, to tell your story. Use at least four frames.
Write your idea for each frame.

Frame 1	Frame 2
Frame 3	Frame 4

Circle the numbers of two or three frames where you can add some fantastic details.

Now draw your comic book on two pieces of paper.

Check Your Work

- ☐ I drew an amazing story.
- ☐ My story has true details and fantastic details.
- ☐ I can explain which parts are true and which parts are made up.

Name

Good News!

Cut out and paste the sentence parts in the newspaper story in the order they happened.

MAN SAVES AFRICAN PLAIN

1

For a long time, there was no rain on Kapiti Plain.

During this time,

2

One day,

Next,

After that,

Then the arrow hit the cloud and loosed the rain.

3

At last,

Ki-pat shot the arrow at the cloud.

the cows were hungry and dry.

the rain fell on the dry plain.

Ki-pat made an arrow from the feather.

an eagle dropped a feather.

Adding Endings

Write the base word and ending for each underlined word.

1 The man was <u>named</u> Ki-pat.

_____ _____
base word   ending

2 Ki-pat <u>looked</u> at the sky often.

_____ _____
base word   ending

3 He was <u>hoping</u> for rain.

_____ _____
base word   ending

4 An eagle <u>dropped</u> a feather.

_____ _____
base word   ending

5 It had been <u>flapping</u> its wings.

_____ _____
base word   ending

Read each sentence. Add **ed** or **ing** to the base word in ( ).
Write the new word to complete the sentence.

6 Giraffes were _____ fast across the plain. (run)

7 Animals _____ to the river for a drink. (race)

8 The cows _____ for water. (moo)

9 Ki-pat was _____. (smile)

10 The rain _____ off the grass. (drip)

Tell Me a Tale   **91**

Name _____

Greetings!

Send this post card home from Kapiti Plain. Use
words from the box to complete each sentence.
Write your name at the bottom of the card.

wild
cloud
stood
happen
heavy
rain
change

Dear Friends,

The sky here is filled with a huge

_____. But it is very dry here

because there is no _____. All of the

_____ animals have gone away to look

for water. I _____ on the plain all day

and did not see even one. I hope that the weather will

_____ soon. The animals may come

back if something will _____ to bring

a _____ rain.

Love,

Name

Picture a Poem

Cut out and paste the pictures in the boxes to complete a poem. Then read the poem aloud. Listen for the rhyme.

The ☐ was as dark as the ☐ .

The ☐ was bright like the ☐ .

The ☐ fell like ☐ .

A tropical storm had begun!

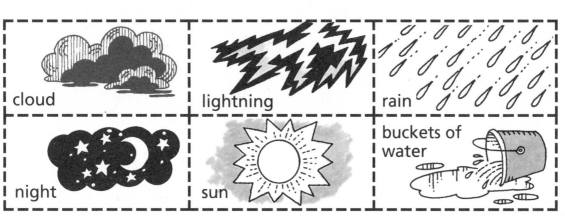

| cloud | lightning | rain |
| night | sun | buckets of water |

From the Top

Look carefully at the picture. Then color it. Write
sentences to describe the picture from top to bottom.

_____

_____

_____

_____

_____

_____

Name _____

Happy Endings

Each Spelling Word is made up of a base word and the ending **ed** or **ing**. The base word ends with a short vowel sound followed by a consonant. The final consonant in each base word is doubled before **ed** or **ing** is added.

drop + p + ed ➜ drop**ped**

get + t + ing ➜ get**ting**

Double the final consonant of the base word to finish each Spelling Word. Write the letter on the hut. Then write the words.

1. clap _____ ed   3. hug _____ ing   5. shop _____ ing   7. get _____ ing

2. sit _____ ing   4. drop _____ ed   6. step _____ ed   8. stop _____ ed

① _____   ⑤ _____

② _____   ⑥ _____

③ _____   ⑦ _____

④ _____   ⑧ _____

Which two Spelling Words have the short **e** sound in the base word?

⑨ _____   ⑩ _____

Spelling Spree

Write Spelling Words to complete
the sentences in this play.

Spelling Words

1. **dropped**   5. **sitting**
2. **clapped**   6. **stepped**
3. **getting**   7. **hugging**
4. **stopped**   8. **shopping**

Zebra: Did you see what happened when it started to rain?

Giraffe: Children ___(1)___ their hands and cheered.

Eagle: Farmers walked around kissing and ___(2)___ their cows.

Leopard: The women who were ___(3)___ for food ___(4)___ their
bags on the ground and began to dance.

Zebra: People sure are funny!

1 _____   **3** _____

2 _____   **4** _____

Find and circle four Spelling Words that are spelled wrong
in this journal. Then write each word correctly.

Tuesday

My friend and I have just stept out of the hut.

The rain has finally stoped. The sky is gitting

lighter. A herd of cows is sittin in the tall grass.

Tomorrow I will look for my bow. I think I

dropped it near an acacia tree.

5 _____

6 _____

7 _____

8 _____

Name _____

Big Plain

Write adjectives on the lines to describe the things in the picture. Use the words from the box.

black	long	large
fresh	round	thin

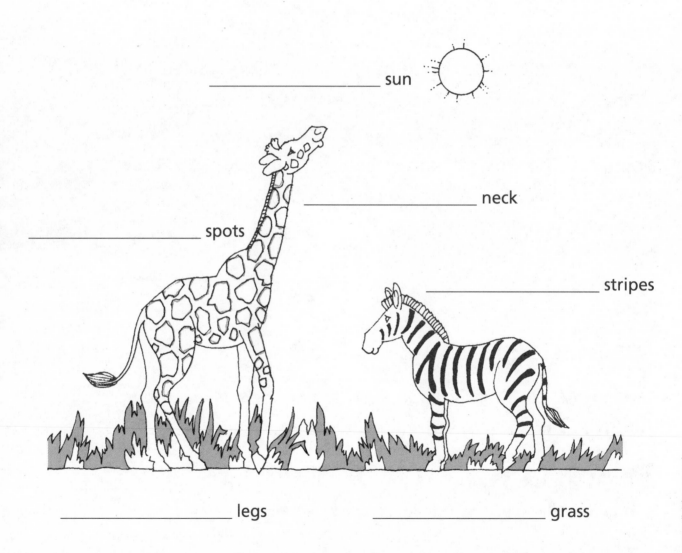

_____ sun

_____ neck

_____ spots

_____ stripes

_____ legs   _____ grass

Write a sentence about the picture. Use two adjectives.

_____

_____

Name

Step Right Up!

Look at the drawing and follow the directions.

① Draw a circle around the birds that are identical.

② Draw one line under what the magician has pulled out of the pot.

③ Draw a star next to the person who has just enough money.

④ Circle the person who has exactly twice as much as he needs.

⑤ Draw two lines under the person who is too poor to pay.

Answer the questions.

⑥ What would you double if you could? _____

⑦ How do you show that you're excited? _____

⑧ What is something most people do quickly? _____

Mrs. Haktak's Diary

Complete the entries from Mrs. Haktak's diary to tell about **Two of Everything**.

Sunday

I wish we weren't so _____. The only food we

have comes from _____.

Monday

A lucky day! Mr. Haktak found a magic _____ in the garden.

Whatever you put inside it _____!

So we kept putting in _____

_____.

Tuesday

Today was very strange. I lost my balance and _____

_____. First, Mr. Haktak

pulled me out, and then he pulled out _____

_____. Next, Mr. Haktak

fell in, so now there are _____.

Name _____

Matching Pairs

Draw a line from the event in the top row to the event that happens because of it in the bottom row.

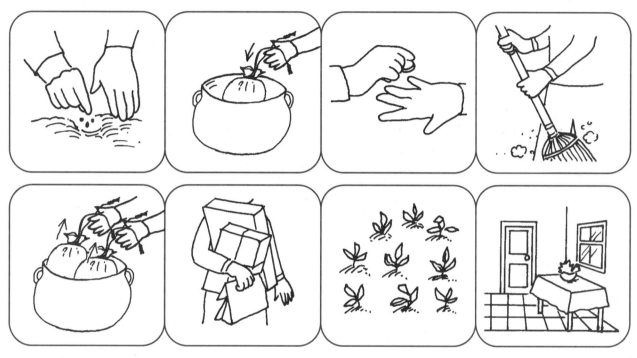

Complete each sentence so that it gives a cause and an effect.

CAUSE	EFFECT
Mr. Haktak _____ seeds.	Plants _____.
Mr. Haktak pays _____.	He can _____ things.
Mrs. Haktak _____.	She has a _____ house.
Mrs. Haktak puts a _____ in the pot.	She has _____ purses.

A Pot Full of Rhymes

Write a word from the box
that rhymes with each word in
the pot.

boy	real	nose
voice	noise	foil
royal	toast	join

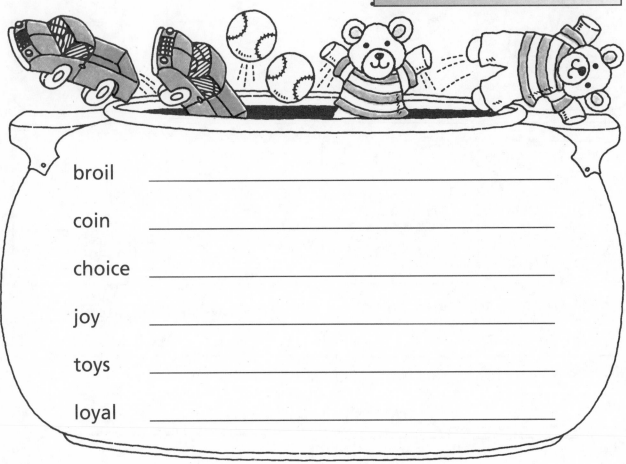

broil   _____

coin   _____

choice   _____

joy   _____

toys   _____

loyal   _____

Now write two sentences. In each sentence, use a word
from the pot.

_____

_____

_____

Interview with Mr. Haktak

Choose words from the box to complete the questions.
Write the answers Mr. Haktak might give.

| enough   person   poor   quickly |

1 **Question:** What did you wish for when you were

_____? **Answer:**_____

_____.

2 **Question:** How _____ did you

learn to pull things out of the pot? **Answer:** _____

_____.

3 **Question:** Were you excited to see a _____

just like yourself? What did you say to him? **Answer:** _____

_____.

4 **Question:** When you have _____

of everything, what will you do? **Answer:** _____

_____.

....

Name

Big Pot, Little Pots

Read each sentence. Choose the word in the big pot
that means almost the same thing as the underlined
word. Write the word.

1 Mr. Haktak <u>found</u> a magic pot in his garden. _____

2 "The pot looks <u>old</u>," said Mr. Haktak. _____

3 It was almost too <u>big</u> for him to carry home. _____

4 Mrs. Haktak was <u>happy</u> with the pot. _____

5 "We can <u>throw</u> coins into it," she

said. _____

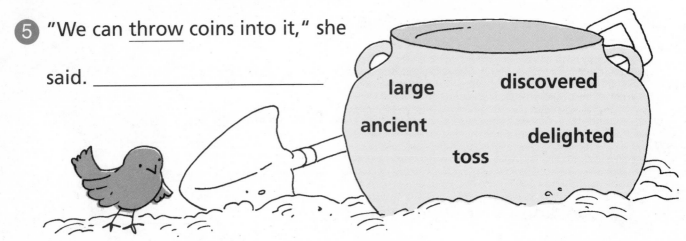

large   discovered

ancient   delighted

toss

Read the word in each little pot and write a
word that means almost the same.

tasty

smart

sleepy

run

choose

Name _____

Seeing Double

What would you like to have two of? Draw pictures
of some things you would put in the pot.

Describe each thing you drew, using clear adjectives.

_____

_____

_____

_____

_____

Double or Nothing

1. **joy**	5. **join**
2. **coin**	6. **boy**
3. **oil**	7. **spoil**
4. **toy**	8. **boil**

Name

Each Spelling Word has the vowel sound that you hear in **boy**. This vowel sound may be spelled **oi** or **oy**.

the vowel sound in boy → coin, joy

 Your Own Words

Write the missing letters to make Spelling Words. Then write each word on the purse that has the same spelling for the vowel sound in **boy**.

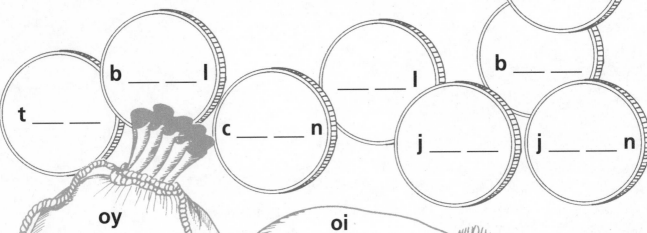

sp __ __ l

b __ __ l

__ __ l

b __ __ __

t __ __

c __ __ n

j __ __

j __ __ n

oy

1 _____

2 _____

3 _____

oi

4 _____

5 _____

6 _____

7 _____

8 _____

Write Spelling Words to answer the questions.

9 Which word begins and ends like **can**? _____

10 Which word begins like **speak**? _____

Spelling Spree

Write a Spelling Word to finish each riddle. Then see if you can think of the answer to each riddle.

Spelling Words	
1. **joy**	5. **join**
2. **coin**	6. **boy**
3. **oil**	7. **spoil**
4. **toy**	8. **boil**

1. Why do we dress a baby _____ in blue?

2. Where would a fish put a gold _____?

3. What group did the rabbit _____ when it grew up?

4. Where can you always find a game or a _____?

1 _____

2 _____

3 _____

4 _____

Find and circle four Spelling Words that are spelled wrong in this note. Then write each word correctly.

Dear Mrs. Chang,

  We are jumping for joi! Now nothing can spoile our fun. We did not find oyl in our yard. Instead we found a pot. We cannot boile water in it. But when we put one coin in the pot, we pull out two. We are rich!

      Mr. and Mrs. Haktak

5 _____

6 _____

7 _____

8 _____

Riddle Answers:
1. because he can't dress himself
2. in a riverbank
3. the hare force
4. in the yellow pages

Name _____

Boiling Over

Count the things in each pot. Write an adjective that
tells how many.

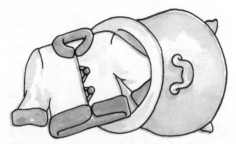

1 _____ coat

4 _____ purses

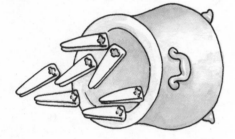

2 _____ hairpins

5 _____ hens

3 _____ teapots

6 _____ coins

Now write a sentence about what you would like to pull out
of the pot. Use an adjective that tells **how many**.

7 _____

_____

Five-Senses Chart

Think of sense words to use in your description.
Write the words in the chart.

 Sight

 Sound

Smell

 Taste

Feel

Name _____

Check It Out!

• Revising Checklist •

Ask yourself these questions about your description.

☐ Do I use sense words to tell about how something looks, feels, tastes, sounds, or smells?

☐ Do I use details so that someone can picture it?

☐ Is there anything I want to add to my description?

_____

_____

_____

_____

Questions to Ask My Writing Partner

• Can you picture what I am describing?

• Is there anything that is not clear?

• Is there anything I should add?

• What do you like best about my description?

Name _____

A Great Gift

Cut out the shapes at the bottom of the page. Paste them where
they belong to tell the story. Write an ending to the story. Then
decorate the border around the story with different colors.

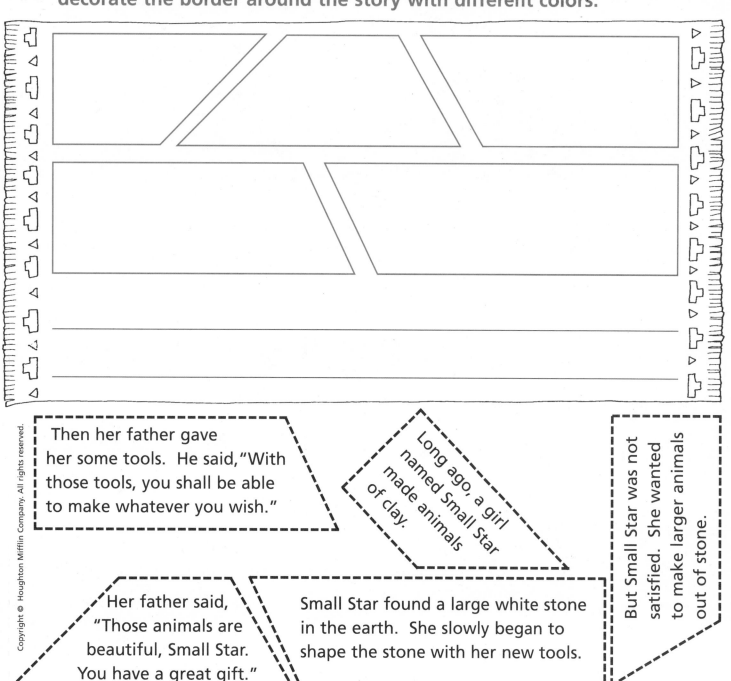

Then her father gave
her some tools. He said, "With
those tools, you shall be able
to make whatever you wish."

Long ago, a girl
named Small Star
made animals
of clay.

But Small Star was not
satisfied. She wanted
to make larger animals
out of stone.

Her father said,
"Those animals are
beautiful, Small Star.
You have a great gift."

Small Star found a large white stone
in the earth. She slowly began to
shape the stone with her new tools.

Name

Hidden Message

Use the clues to complete the puzzle.

1 A Dream - _____ came to Little Gopher when he went to the hills alone.

2 The maiden showed Little Gopher a white _____ .

3 Little Gopher painted scenes of great _____ and great deeds.

4 He wanted to paint _____ that were bright and beautiful.

5 Little Gopher found _____ filled with paint on the hillside.

6 The brushes took root and became colorful _____ .

1. ____ ____ ▮ ____ ____ ____

2. ____ ____ ____ ▮ ____ ____ ____ ____ ____

3. ____ ____ ▮ ____ ____

4. ____ ____ ____ ▮ ____ ____

5. ____ ____ ____ ▮ ____ ____

6. ____ ____ ▮ ____ ____

Write the letters from the boxes to find out what Little Gopher

painted on the buckskin. ____ ____ ____ ____ ____ ____

Tell Me a Tale **113**

Name

What Will Little Gopher Do?

Read each page of Little Gopher's diary.
Think about what you know about him from
the story. Then answer each question.

The warriors asked me to go on the hunt today. It would be fun to go. But a voice in my dream told me to gather red berries to make paint.

What do you think Little Gopher will do?

_____

Why do you think so?

_____

_____

_____

Last night the leader of our people had a Dream-Vision about talking to an eagle. He told me all about it.

What do you think Little Gopher will do?

_____

Why do you think so?

_____

_____

_____

Name

Painted Endings

Look at the base word on the brush and
the ending on the drop of paint. Put
them together to make a new word and
write it on a bowl. Cut and paste the
bowl under the paintbrush that matches.

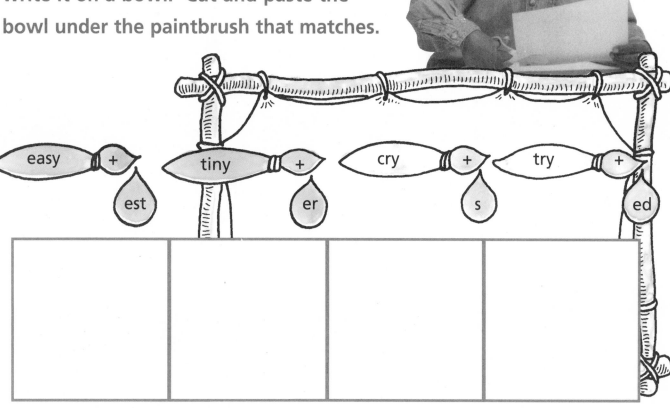

easy + est

tiny + er

cry + s

try + ed

On the back of this page, write two sentences. Use a word
from one of the bowls in each sentence. →

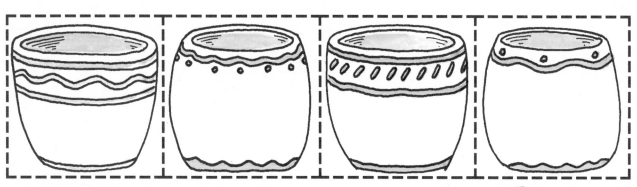

Write two sentences. Use a word from one of the bowls
in each sentence.

1 _____

_____

2 _____

_____

Name

A Legend

Cut out the cloud shapes. Paste the words where they belong.
On the back of this page, write an ending for the legend.

Long ⬚ , clouds were white from morning to night.
One day the clouds saw a rainbow. They asked it, "May we use

⬚ colors that make you so pretty?"

   The rainbow said, "The colors do not belong to me. You must ask the sun."

   So the clouds asked, "Sun, will you paint us with all the

⬚ colors of the rainbow?"

   The sun said, "Every morning, I paint the whole ⬚ .

Wait until the end of the day. I ⬚ see what colors I have left."

   The clouds waited. When the day was nearly over, the sun

⬚ painted clouds with red and purple, orange and gold.

| ago | earth | slowly | those | shall | different |

Write an ending for the legend.

And that is why

_____

_____

_____

_____

_____

_____

The Legend of the
Indian Paintbrush
VOCABULARY
Adverbs with -ly

Name

Better Word Pictures!

Look at the underlined action words.
Choose an adverb from the HOW
wheel that tells how the action
might happen. Write the adverb in
the blank.

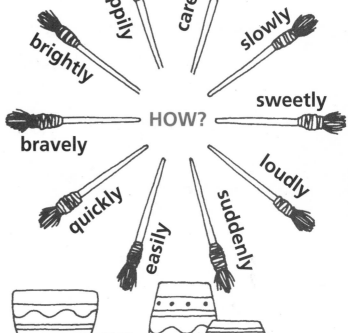

happily   carefully
brightly   slowly
                        sweetly
HOW?
bravely
                        loudly
quickly   suddenly
        easily

1 Little Gopher climbed the mountain _____.

2 The tiny birds sang _____.

3 The wind blew _____.

4 Little Gopher saw his Dream-Vision _____.

5 He walked back to his village _____.

6 Little Gopher painted the picture _____.

7 The sunset glowed _____.

8 Little Gopher laughed _____.

Name _____

The Great Flower Contest

small, smaller, smallest   **big, bigger, biggest**

Imagine there was a contest to pick the prettiest
flower of all. Write a legend to tell about how the
littlest flower on the hill won the contest.
Use **er** and **est** words
to compare things
in your legend.

young, younger, youngest

happy, happier, happiest

pretty, prettier, prettiest

smart, smarter, smartest

_____

_____

_____

_____

_____

_____

_____

brave, braver, bravest   **tall, taller, tallest**

Paint a Picture

Each Spelling Word is made up of a base
word and the ending **ed** or **ing**. The base
word has the vowel-consonant-**e** pattern.
The final **e** in the base word is dropped
before **ed** or **ing** is added.

Spelling Words

1. **making**	5. **placed**
2. **used**	6. **shared**
3. **faded**	7. **riding**
4. **taking**	8. **liked**

 Your Own Words

use – e + ed ➜ used

make – e + ing ➜ making

**Cross out the final e in each base word. Then
write a Spelling Word with the letters that are left.**

1. (take) + (ing)   ❶ _____

2. (like) + (ed)   ❷ _____

3. (ride) + (ing)   ❸ _____

4. (use) + (ed)   ❹ _____

5. (share) + (ed)   ❺ _____

6. (make) + (ing)   ❻ _____

7. (fade) + (ed)   ❼ _____

8. (place) + (ed)   ❽ _____

Which two Spelling Words have the long i sound in the base word?

❾ _____   ❿ _____

Name _____

Spelling Spree

Write a Spelling Word for each clue.

1. It rhymes with **hiding**.
   It begins like **rope**.

2. It rhymes with **raced**.
   It begins like **plant**.

3. It rhymes with **baking**.
   It begins like **time**.

4. It rhymes with **waded**.
   It begins like **fire**.

1 _____

2 _____

3 _____

4 _____

Find and circle four Spelling Words that are spelled wrong in this
speech. Then write each word correctly.

Little Gopher was a great artist. He was
always makeing beautiful things. He always shaired
them with the tribe.

He liket to watch the sun in the evening. Once he
painted a sunset. He uzed the brightest colors.

Even today the colors have not faded.

5 _____

6 _____

7 _____

8 _____

Name _____

Ride a Painted Pony

Choose a word from the word box to finish each sentence.

| fast |
| faster |
| fastest |

The gray horse is fast.

1 The spotted horse is _____ than the gray horse.

2 The black horse is the _____ of all.

| short |
| shorter |
| shortest |

Russ is short.

3 Jimmy is _____ than Russ.

4 Willy is the _____ of the three boys.

Name

Old Story, New Story

Tell an old story in a new way. First, read this chart
about **Two of Everything**.

What happens	What makes it happen
Mr. and Mrs. Haktak find a pot.	Mr. Haktak digs it up.
They learn what the pot does.	One hairpin becomes two hairpins.
They use it to get what they want.	They put money in the pot.
Then they get two new people.	Mr and Mrs. Haktak fall into the pot.
At the end, everyone is happy.	They have everything they want.

Now use the same ideas, in the same order, to tell your story.

What happens	What makes it happen
My characters find	
They learn that it can	
They use it to	
Then	
At the end,	

Write your story.   ☐ My story is a new way of telling an old story.

Check your work.   ☐ It keeps the same order of events.

☐ It tells why things happen the way they do.

MORE
SPELLING
PRACTICE

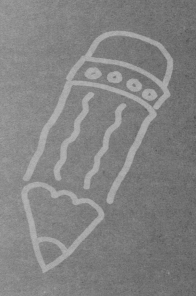

MORE SPELLING PRACTICE

Contents

Picture Perfect

These Spelling Words are words that you use in your writing. Look carefully at how they are spelled.

Use the Spelling Words to complete the sentences. Write the words in the photo frames.

1. We needed ____ more paper for our photo album.

2. We had a lot of pictures to put ____ it.

3. Finally, our photo album was ____ .

4. There was ____ photo of the twins on their bikes.

5. There were a few pictures of you and ____ brother.

6. I put the ____ best pictures of Miriam and me in too.

7. We pasted a group photo on the ____ cover.

8. No one knew the name of one ____ in the picture.

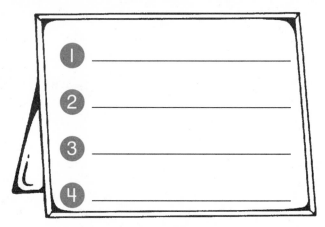

9. Which Spelling Word begins with the first sound you hear in 🦕 ?

10. Which Spelling Word begins with the first sound you hear in 🦭 ?

Name _____

Spelling Spree

Write a Spelling Word to finish each silly
riddle. Can you guess each answer?

1 Why did the _____ throw a
clock on her bed?

2 What has four legs and a _____ but no body?

3 What happens when you throw a green rock

_____ the Red Sea?

4 How can you double _____ money?

Find and circle four Spelling Words that are spelled
wrong in this story. Then write each word correctly.

   Last night at supper I ate wun ear of corn. My sister,
Sara, ate too ears of corn. I had three carrots. Sara
had six. Then we did our homework. We had som math
problems. When we were dun, we had a snack. I ate three
figs, and Sara ate six. Then I thought about what Sara and
I eat. Sara eats twice as much as I do.

5 _____   7 _____

6 _____   8 _____

Name

Spelling Review

Write Spelling Words from the list on this page to answer the questions.

Spelling Words

car	foot
book	corn
under	after
noon	start
for	more

Your Own Words

 the vowel sound ➜ soon

the 📖 vowel sound ➜ look

1. Which word has the 🌙 vowel sound?

2–3. Which two words have the 📖 vowel sound?

① _____   ② _____   ③ _____

the vowel + r sound in hard ➜ ar

4–5. Which two words have the vowel + **r** sound spelled **ar**?

④ _____   ⑤ _____

the vowel + r sound in store ➜ or, ore

6–7. Which two words have the vowel + **r** sound spelled **or**?

8. Which word has the vowel + **r** sound spelled **ore**?

⑥ _____   ⑦ _____   ⑧ _____

the vowel + r sound in father ➜ er

9–10. Which two words end with the vowel + **r** sound spelled **er**?

⑨ _____

⑩ _____

Name

Spelling Spree

Write the Spelling Word that answers
the question and rhymes with the word
in **dark print**.

Example: What is a container for candy

called? a candy **bar** __jar__

Spelling Words	
dark	girl
your	store
better	jar
room	back
into	brother

1. What is a shop near the sea called? a **shore** ____
2. What is a place for brushes called? a **broom** ____
3. What is a more than good hunting dog called? a ____ **setter**
4. What is a playground at night called? a ____ **park**
5. What is a railroad behind a house called? a ____ **track**
6. What is a dance step made by a lady called? a ____ **twirl**

1 _____   3 _____   5 _____

2 _____   4 _____   6 _____

Find and circle four Spelling Words that are spelled
wrong in this story. Then write each word correctly.

    I lost my tooth today. When I told my
bruther, Tom, he took it and put it in a jur.
"It's not yowr tooth, it's mine!" I said.
"Give it back!" Then Mom yelled. Now
Tom cannot watch TV for a week. He can
always get ento trouble.

7 _____

8 _____

9 _____

10 _____

Amazing Animals

These Spelling Words are words that you use in your writing. Look carefully at how they are spelled.

Use the Spelling Words to complete the sentences. Write the words in the fish.

Spelling Words

1. **who**	5. **our**
2. **a lot**	6. **friend**
3. **were**	7. **cannot**
4. **many**	8. **here**

 Your Own Words

1. There are ____ ____ of amazing animals.
2. The pictures in ____ book show a few.
3. I have ____ pictures of fish.
4. I ____ show them all to you today.
5. I wonder ____ named the porcupine fish.
6. Is this a picture of it ____?
7. The eels ____ hiding in the seaweed.
8. The eel is not a ____ of the octopus.

1 _____
2 _____
3 _____
4 _____

5 _____
6 _____

7 _____
8 _____

9. Which Spelling Word begins with a consonant cluster?

10. Which Spelling Word begins with the first sound you hear in  spelled **wh**?

9 _____

10 _____

Name _____

Spelling Spree

Use the Spelling Words to complete the
sentences. Write the words in the puzzle.

Spelling Words	
1. **who**	5. **our**
2. **a lot**	6. **friend**
3. **were**	7. **cannot**
4. **many**	8. **here**

Across

1. Do you know _____ wanted the book
   about the elephant bird?

4. Did you sit with your ____?

Down

2. Read about the animal in _____ book.

3. Please put the book ____.

Find and circle four Spelling Words that are spelled
wrong in this report. Then write each word correctly.

> The elephant bird was about ten feet
> tall and looked ulot like the ostrich. The
> elephant bird could not fly. It was too big
> and heavy, and its wings wer small. Long
> ago, people found out that this bird was
> good to eat. They killed so meny elephant
> birds that today none are alive. You canot
> find even one.

5  _____   7  _____

6 _____   8  _____

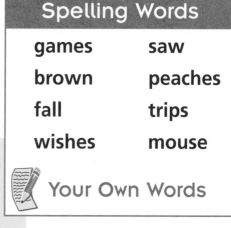

Spelling Review

Write Spelling Words from the list on this
page to answer the questions.

games	saw
brown	peaches
fall	trips
wishes	mouse

 Your Own Words

Add **s** to most words to name
more than one.
Add **es** to words that end with
s, **x**, **sh**, or **ch** to name more than one.

1-2. Which two words have the **s** ending to name
more than one?

3-4. Which two words have the **es** ending to name
more than one?

① _____   ③ _____

② _____   ④ _____

 the

the cow vowel sound → down, house

5. Which word has the cow vowel sound spelled **ow**?
6. Which word has the cow vowel sound spelled **ou**?

⑤ _____   ⑥ _____

 the

the ball vowel sound → draw, small

7. Which word has the ball vowel sound spelled **aw**?
8. Which word has the ball vowel sound spelled **a** before **ll**?

⑦    ⑧

Name

Spelling Spree

Write the Spelling Word from the list on
this page that fits each clue.

1. the foot of a dog ____ ____ ◯

2. a home ◯ ____ ____ ____ ____

3. a large number ____ ◯ ____ ____

4. groups of students ____ ◯ ____ ____ ____ ____ ____

5. a person whom
   you know and like ____ ____ ◯ ____ ____ ____

Now write the circled letters
in order. They spell the name
of the largest living animal.

the blue ____ ____ ____ ____

Find and circle three Spelling Words that are spelled
wrong in this report. Then write each word correctly.

The house mouse builds its nest in houses and barns.
The animal is very smol. It has a long tail and
whiskers. It can hear well, but it kinnot see very well.
Before 1500, there were no mice hir. They came to
North and South America on ships from Europe.

 6 ____   7 ____   8 ____

Feathers of Many Colors

These Spelling Words are words that you use in your writing. Look carefully at how they are spelled.

Use the Spelling Words to complete the sentences. Write the words in the barn.

Spelling Words	
1. **tried**	5. **new**
2. **never**	6. **very**
3. **going**	7. **other**
4. **coming**	8. **started**

Your Own Words

1. The rooster's coat was colorful and ____.
2. The coat was ____ pretty.
3. The fox had ____ seen one like it before.
4. The fox is ____ away with the coat.
5. When will he be ____ back?
6. The rooster ____ to worry when the fox didn't come back.
7. The rooster couldn't call him in any ____ way than by crowing.
8. He ____ to bring back the fox by crowing.

1 ____
2 ____
3 ____
4 ____
5 ____
6 ____
7 ____
8 ____

9. In which Spelling Word was the final **e** of the base word dropped before **ing** was added?

10. In which Spelling Word was the final **y** of the base word changed to **i** before **ed** was added?

9 ____

10 ____

Name _____

Spelling Spree

Find and circle four Spelling Words that are spelled wrong in this story. Then write each word correctly.

Spelling Words	
1. **tried**	5. **new**
2. **never**	6. **very**
3. **going**	7. **other**
4. **coming**	8. **started**

My dog, Molly, has big brown eyes and fluffy white fur. She is verre small, but she likes to chase all kinds of animals. One day we were gowing for a walk. A big dog started comming toward us. Molly tryd to run after it, but it chased her. Molly jumped into my arms. Now she won't chase anything!

1 _____   3 _____

2 _____   4 _____

Write the Spelling Word for each clue.

5. A word that rhymes with **stew** and means "not old" is ____.

6. A word that rhymes with **parted** and means "began" is ____.

7. A word that rhymes with **clever** and means "not ever" is ____.

8. A word that rhymes with **brother** and means "a different one" is ____.

5 _____

6 _____

7 _____

8 _____

Spelling Review

Write Spelling Words from the list on this page to answer the questions.

Spelling Words	
toy	coin
shared	shopping
clapped	riding
making	boil

 Your Own Words

step + p + ed → step**ped**

get + t + ing → get**ting**

1–2. In which two words was the final consonant of the base word doubled before **ed** or **ing** was added?

① _____   ② _____

the vowel sound in b**oy** → sp**oi**l, j**oy**

3. Which word has the vowel sound in **boy** spelled **oy**?

4–5. Which two words have the vowel sound in **boy** spelled **oi**?

③ _____   ⑤ _____

④ _____

like – e + ed → lik**ed**

ride – e + ing → rid**ing**

6–8. In which three words was the final **e** dropped from the base word before **ed** or **ing** was added?

⑥ _____   ⑧ _____

⑦ _____

Name

Spelling Spree

Write the Spelling Word from the list on this page that means the opposite of each word.

1. girl _____

2. always _____

3. hated _____

4. old _____

5. standing _____

6. finished _____

Find and circle four Spelling Words that are spelled wrong in this story. Then write each word correctly.

The uther day my little brother, Julio, was siting on the front steps. He was wearing a new shirt and pants. "I'm waiting for Mom," he said. Just then, two cats that had been running in the mud stopd and jumped onto his lap. Mom will nevar believe that he wasn't playing in the mud.

7. _____

8. _____

9. _____

10. _____

Name

Two Alike

Each Spelling Word is a homophone for another word on the list. **Homophones** are words that sound alike but do not have the same spelling or the same meaning.

 week   A **week** is an amount of time. One week is seven days.

 weak   **Weak** is the opposite of strong.

Write the Spelling Word that fits each clue. Then draw a circle around each pair of homophones.

1. I start on Sunday.
2. I cannot lift a big box.
3. I am another word for **important**.
4. I am found on the back of a horse's neck.
5. A cat or a dog has one.
6. I am a kind of story.
7. Use me when you dig up sand.
8. I am the opposite of **bright**.

1 _____
2 _____
3 _____
4 _____
5 _____
6 _____
7 _____
8 _____

Take-Home Word Lists

Homophones
Homophones are words that sound alike but do not have the same spelling or the same meaning.

week   weak

Spelling Words
1. week
2. weak
3. pail
4. pale
5. tail
6. tale
7. main
8. mane

Challenge Words
1. blue
2. blew

My Study List
Add your own spelling words on the back. →

Take-Home Word Lists

Name _____

 My Study List

1. _____

2. _____

3. _____

4. _____

5. _____

6. _____

7. _____

8. _____

Additional Spelling Words

1. see   3. so

2. sea   4. sew

How to Study a Word

LOOK at the word.

SAY the word.

THINK about the word.

WRITE the word.

CHECK the spelling.

 140

Name _____

Spelling Spree

Think how the words in each group are alike. Write the missing Spelling Words.

Spelling Words	
1. **week**	5. **tail**
2. **weak**	6. **tale**
3. **pail**	7. **main**
4. **pale**	8. **mane**

1. nose, paw,

2. day, month,

3. bucket, tub,

4. hoof, leg,

① _____

② _____

③ _____

④ _____

Find and circle four Spelling Words that are spelled wrong in this book report. Then write each word correctly.

The Castaway by Sam Bent is a true story, not a tail. A man was on a ship that sank. He swam to a land where no one lived. His mane food was coconuts. He got thin and pail. Each week he watched for a ship. At last he saw one. He was weke, but he swam to the ship and was saved.

⑤ _____   ⑦ _____

⑥ _____   ⑧ _____

Name

Happy Puppy

Each Spelling Word has two parts, called **syllables**. Each syllable has one vowel sound. You hear the long **e** sound in the second syllable of each word. In these words, the long **e** sound is spelled **y**.

long e sound → pup py   par ty

Write the correct syllable from the bone to complete each Spelling Word.

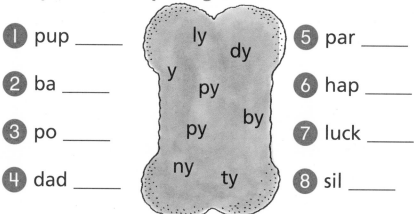

① pup _____

② ba _____

③ po _____

④ dad _____

⑤ par _____

⑥ hap _____

⑦ luck _____

⑧ sil _____

(bone contains: ly dy y py by py ny ty)

Now write each word. Draw a line under the letter that spells the long **e** sound in each word.

⑨ _____

⑩ _____

⑪ _____

⑫ _____

⑬ _____

⑭ _____

⑮ _____

⑯ _____

Final Sound in **puppy**

long **e** sound → **y**

pupp**y**   part**y**

Spelling Words
1. puppy
2. party
3. silly
4. pony
5. baby
6. lucky
7. happy
8. daddy

Challenge Words
1. noisy
2. furry

My Study List

Add your own spelling words on the back. →

Take-Home Word Lists

Name _____

 My Study List

1. _____

2. _____

3. _____

4. _____

5. _____

6. _____

7. _____

8. _____

Additional Spelling Words

1. muddy   3. study

2. sticky   4. lady

How to Study a Word

LOOK at the word.

SAY the word.

THINK about the word.

WRITE the word.

CHECK the spelling.

142

Name ·····················

Spelling Spree

Write the Spelling Word that answers each question and rhymes with the word in **dark print**.

Spelling Words	
1. **puppy**	5. **baby**
2. **party**	6. **lucky**
3. **silly**	7. **happy**
4. **pony**	8. **daddy**

1 What is a thin horse? a **bony** _____

2 What is a bird with a prize? a _____ **ducky**

3 What is a foolish goat? a _____ **billy**

4 What is a glad father? a _____ **pappy**

Find and circle four Spelling Words that are spelled wrong in this part of a letter. Then write each word correctly.

> Dear Josh,
>   Yesterday Ellen put babe clothes on our pupy. She put a hat on his head. Then she sat him in a highchair. She said she was having a tea partey. She asked our dady and me to come. I felt so silly. It's hard to have a little sister!

5 _____   7 _____

6 _____   8 _____

142 **More Spelling Practice**

Two Words in One

Each Spelling Word is a compound word.
A **compound word** is made up of two
shorter words.

mail + box = **mailbox**

Draw a line to connect the two words that
make up each Spelling Word. The first one is
done for you. Then write the Spelling Words.

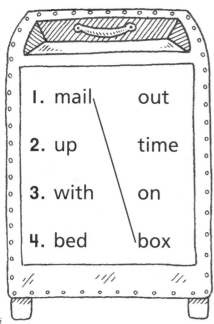

1. mail   out
2. up   time
3. with   on
4. bed   box

5. pan   paste
6. pea   cake
7. may   nut
8. tooth   be

1 _____

2 _____

3 _____

4 _____

5 _____

6 _____

7 _____

8 _____

Take-Home Word Lists

Compound Words

mail + box = **mailbox**

pea + nut = **peanut**

Spelling Words

1. mailbox
2. peanut
3. without
4. pancake
5. bedtime
6. maybe
7. upon
8. toothpaste

Challenge Words

1. sweatshirt
2. downstairs

My Study List

Add your own spelling
words on the back. →

143

Name _____

 My Study List

1. _____

2. _____

3. _____

4. _____

5. _____

6. _____

7. _____

8. _____

Additional Spelling Words

1. doghouse

2. backpack

3. footprint

4. grasshopper

How to Study a Word

LOOK at the word.

SAY the word.

THINK about the word.

WRITE the word.

CHECK the spelling.

Name _____

Spelling Spree

Write the Spelling Word for each clue.

1. You put me on your toothbrush.

2. I am good to eat for breakfast.

3. You make a kind of butter with me.

4. I mean "on top of."

① _____ ③ _____

② _____ ④ _____

Find and circle four Spelling Words that are spelled wrong in this ad. Then write each word correctly.

Kitty Cat Toothpaste

You always brush your teeth before bedtim. Why make your cat go witout brushing? Send us this ad to get a tube of toothpaste in your malbox. Then mabe your cat's teeth will shine!

⑤ _____ ⑦ _____

⑥ _____ ⑧ _____

Tap the Speller

How to play

Players 4 or more, with one player at a time the caller

You need

• list of Spelling Words

Getting ready

Choose the first caller. Sit in a circle with the other players, except for the caller.

Each player tries to become the caller by spelling a word correctly.

1. The caller reads a Spelling Word aloud and begins walking around the circle.

2. The caller taps a player on the shoulder. The player spells the word. If the spelling is correct, that player becomes the caller.

3. If the spelling is not correct, the caller taps another player to spell the same word.

4. The game goes on until every player has had a chance to be the caller.

Catch the Bus

How to play

Players 2 or more and a caller

You need

- list of Spelling Words
- game board from page 147
- game marker for each player
- spinner

Getting ready

Draw a spinner like the one in the picture below. Use a paper clip as the arrow. Hold the paper clip in place with a pencil tip.

Each player tries to be the first to reach the Bus Stop by spelling words correctly.

1. The caller reads a Spelling Word aloud. Player 1 spells the word.

2. If the spelling is correct, Player 1 spins and moves on the board the number of spaces shown on the spinner. If the spelling is not correct, the caller spells the word aloud correctly.

3. Players must follow any directions in the spaces they land on. If a player lands on a shortcut, he or she can move to the end of the shortcut.

4. Players take turns spelling words and moving along the board. The caller may use misspelled words again. The first player to reach the Bus Stop wins.

Catch ^the Bus

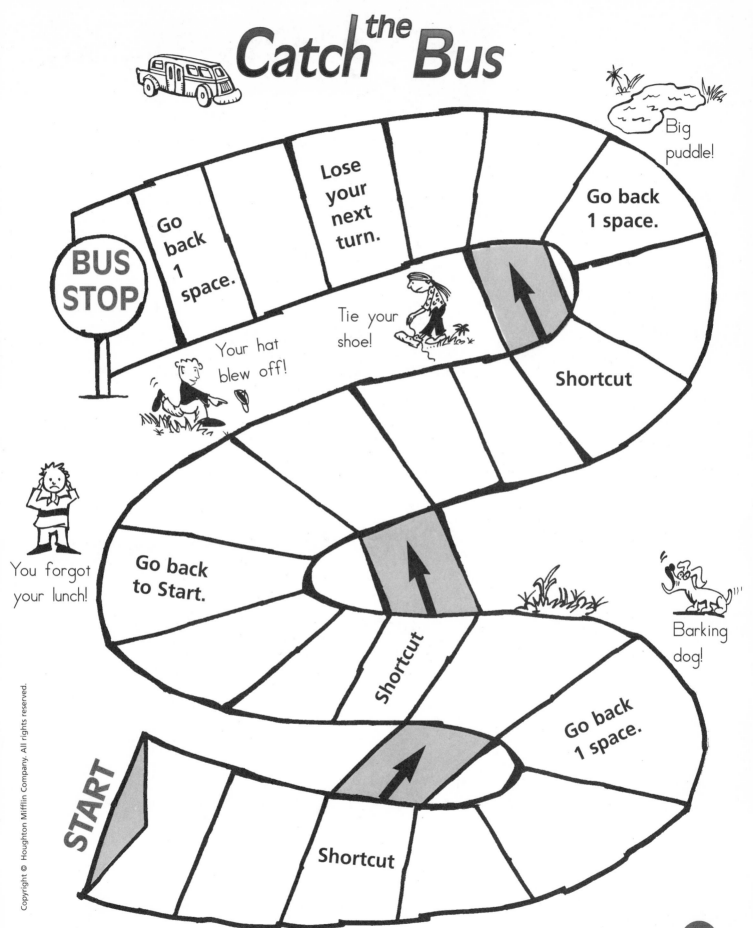

BUS STOP

Go back 1 space.

Lose your next turn.

Big puddle!

Go back 1 space.

Your hat blew off!

Tie your shoe!

Shortcut

You forgot your lunch!

Go back to Start.

Shortcut

Barking dog!

Go back 1 space.

START

Shortcut

Don't P●p the Balloon!

How to play

Players 2 teams of 3 or more and a caller

You need
- list of Spelling Words
- chalkboard
- chalk and eraser

Getting ready

On the chalkboard, draw a bunch of balloons for each team. Draw one balloon for each team member.

Each player tries to spell words correctly to help his or her team keep all their balloons.

1. The caller reads a Spelling Word aloud. A player from Team 1 writes the word in a balloon.

2. If the word is spelled correctly, the balloon stays in the bunch. If the word is not spelled correctly, the caller spells it aloud correctly. The balloon then "pops" and the player erases the balloon.

3. Teams take turns spelling words. When every player has had a turn, the team with the most balloons wins.

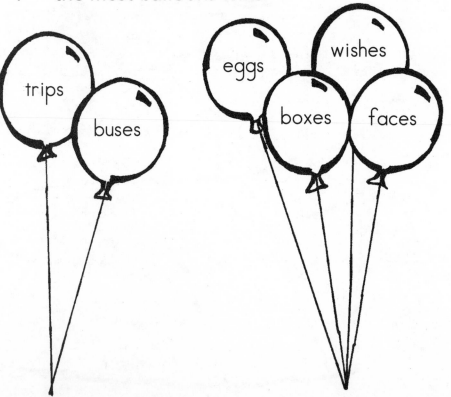

MY
HANDBOOK

Contents

Use this log to record the books you read on your own.

Name of Book _____

Author _____

This book is about _____

_____

_____

_____

Name of Book _____

Author _____

This book is about _____

_____

_____

_____

Name of Book _____

Author _____

This book is about _____

_____

_____

_____

Name of Book _____

Author _____

This book is about _____

_____

_____

_____

Name of Book _____

Author _____

This book is about _____

_____

_____

_____

Name of Book _____

Author _____

This book is about _____

_____

_____

_____

Name of Book _____

Author _____

This book is about _____

_____

_____

_____

Name of Book _____

Author _____

This book is about _____

_____

_____

_____

Name of Book _____

Author _____

This book is about _____

_____

_____

_____

Name of Book _____

Author _____

This book is about _____

_____

_____

_____

Name of Book _____

Author _____

This book is about _____

_____

_____

_____

Name of Book _____

Author _____

This book is about _____

_____

_____

_____

Name of Book _____

Author _____

This book is about _____

_____

_____

_____

Name of Book _____

Author _____

This book is about _____

_____

_____

_____

Name of Book _____

Author _____

This book is about _____

_____

_____

_____

Name of Book _____

Author _____

This book is about _____

_____

_____

_____

Name of Book _____

Author _____

This book is about _____

_____

_____

_____

Trace and write the letters.

Aa Aa

Bb Bb

Cc Cc

Dd Dd

Ee Ee

Ff Ff

Gg Gg

HANDWRITING MODELS

Trace and write the letters.

Hh Hh

Ii Ii

Jj Jj

Kk Kk

Ll Ll

Mm Mm

McDougal, Littell 1993 Handwriting

Trace and write the letters.

Nn Nn

Oo Oo

Pp Pp

Qq Qq

Rr Rr

Ss Ss

Tt Tt

Trace and write the letters.

$\mathcal{U}\mathcal{u}$ $\mathcal{U}\mathcal{u}$

$\mathcal{V}\mathcal{v}$ $\mathcal{V}\mathcal{v}$

$\mathcal{W}\mathcal{w}$ $\mathcal{W}\mathcal{w}$

$\mathcal{X}\mathcal{x}$ $\mathcal{X}\mathcal{x}$

$\mathcal{Y}\mathcal{y}$ $\mathcal{Y}\mathcal{y}$

$\mathcal{Z}\mathcal{z}$ $\mathcal{Z}\mathcal{z}$

Trace and write the letters.

Aa Aa

Bb Bb

Cc Cc

Dd Dd

Ee Ee

Ff Ff

Gg Gg

HANDWRITING MODELS

Trace and write the letters.

Hh   Hh

Ii   Ii

Jj   Jj

Kk   Kk

Ll   Ll

Mm   Mm

McDougal, Littell 1990 Handwriting

Trace and write the letters.

Nn Nn

Oo Oo

Pp Pp

Qq Qq

Rr Rr

Ss Ss

Tt Tt

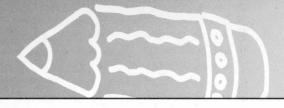

HANDWRITING MODELS

Trace and write the letters.

Uu Uu

Vv Vv

Ww Ww

Xx Xx

Yy Yy

Zz Zz

How to Study a Word

1 LOOK at the word.

- What does the word mean?
- What letters are in the word?
- Name and touch each letter.

2 SAY the word.

- Listen for the consonant sounds.
- Listen for the vowel sounds.

3 THINK about the word.

- How is each sound spelled?
- Close your eyes and picture the word.
- What other words have the same spelling patterns?

4 WRITE the word.

- Think about the sounds and the letters.
- Form the letters correctly.

5 CHECK the spelling.

- Did you spell the word the same way it is spelled in your word list?
- Write the word again if you did not spell it correctly.

SPECIAL WORDS FOR WRITING

A
about
again
a lot
always
am
and
any
are
around
as

B
back
because
been
before

C
cannot
caught
come
coming
could

D
do
does

done
down

E
enough

F
family
first
for
found
friend
from

G
getting
girl
goes
going

H
has
have
heard
her
here
his
how

I
I'd
if
I'll
I'm
into
it
it's

K
knew
know

L
letter
little

M
many
more
my
myself

N
name
never
new
now

O
of
off
on
once
one
other
our
outside

P
people
pretty

R
really
right

S
said
school
some
something
started
stopped

T
that's
the
their
there

they
thought
through
time
to
today
too
tried
two

V
very

W
want
was
went
were
what
when
where
who
will
would
write

Y
you
your

A Chair for My Mother

Vowel + r Sound in car

vowel + r sound ➔ **j**ar

➔ **ar**m

Spelling Words

1. jar
2. arm
3. hard
4. are
5. start
6. car
7. far
8. dark

Challenge Words

1. apart
2. charcoal

My Study List

Add your own spelling words on the back. ➔

Clean Your Room, Harvey Moon!

The Vowel Sounds in

moon **and** book

moon ➔ n**oo**n

book ➔ l**oo**k, f**oo**t

Spelling Words

1. room
2. moon
3. book
4. soon
5. look
6. noon
7. broom
8. foot

Challenge Words

1. cookie
2. cartoon

My Study List

Add your own spelling words on the back. ➔

Name_____

 My Study List

1._____

2._____

3._____

4._____

5._____

6._____

7._____

8._____

Additional Spelling Words

1. pool   **3.** hood

2. loop   **4.** boot

How to Study a Word

LOOK at the word.

SAY the word.

THINK about the word.

WRITE the word.

CHECK the spelling.

168

Name_____

 My Study List

1._____

2._____

3._____

4._____

5._____

6._____

7._____

8._____

Additional Spelling Words

1. park   **3.** yard

2. card   **4.** star

How to Study a Word

LOOK at the word.

SAY the word.

THINK about the word.

WRITE the word.

CHECK the spelling.

168

Now One Foot, Now the Other

Vowel + r Sound in store

vowel + **r** sound ➞ f**or**

➞ m**ore**

Spelling Words

1. for
2. more
3. or
4. story
5. born
6. short
7. store
8. corn

Challenge Words

1. before
2. morning

My Study List

Add your own spelling words on the back. ➞

Family Photos: Reading-Writing Workshop

Look carefully at how these words are spelled.

Spelling Words

1. done
2. one
3. two
4. back
5. some
6. your
7. girl
8. into

Challenge Words

1. knew
2. pretty

My Study List

Add your own spelling words on the back. ➞

Name_____

 My Study List

1. _____
2. _____
3. _____
4. _____
5. _____
6. _____
7. _____
8. _____

Additional Spelling Words

1. once   3. around
2. I'll   4. found

How to Study a Word

LOOK at the word.

SAY the word.

THINK about the word.

WRITE the word.

CHECK the spelling.

Name_____

 My Study List

1. _____
2. _____
3. _____
4. _____
5. _____
6. _____
7. _____
8. _____

Additional Spelling Words

1. horn   3. north
2. horse   4. shore

How to Study a Word

LOOK at the word.

SAY the word.

THINK about the word.

WRITE the word.

CHECK the spelling.

Family Photos: Spelling Review

Spelling Words

1. car
2. book
3. under
4. noon
5. for
6. foot
7. corn
8. after
9. start
10. more
11. dark
12. your
13. better
14. room
15. into
16. girl
17. store
18. jar
19. back
20. brother

See the back for Challenge Words.

My Study List

Add your own spelling words on the back. ➡️

Too Many Tamales

> **Words That End with er**
>
> bett**er**
>
> broth**er**
>
> ov**er**

Spelling Words

1. better
2. after
3. over
4. under
5. mother
6. father
7. sister
8. brother

Challenge Words

1. counter
2. center

My Study List

Add your own spelling words on the back. ➡️

Name_____

 My Study List

1._____

2._____

3._____

4._____

5._____

6._____

7._____

8._____

Additional Spelling Words

1. water   3. winter

2. river   4. summer

How to Study a Word

LOOK at the word.

SAY the word.

THINK about the word.

WRITE the word.

CHECK the spelling.

172

Name_____

 My Study List

1._____

2._____

3._____

4._____

5._____

6._____

7._____

8._____

Challenge Words

1. center   4. knew

2. apart   5. before

3. cartoon

How to Study a Word

LOOK at the word.

SAY the word.

THINK about the word.

WRITE the word.

CHECK the spelling.

172

What Happened to Patrick's Dinosaurs?

The Vowel Sound in cow

ow → h**ow**, d**ow**n

ou → **ou**t, h**ou**se

Spelling Words

1. how
2. out
3. now
4. house
5. down
6. brown
7. cow
8. mouse

Challenge Words

1. about
2. shower

My Study List

Add your own spelling words on the back. →

The Day Jimmy's Boa Ate the Wash

Words That End with

s **or** es

s → trip**s**, face**s**

es → bus**es**, box**es**

wish**es**, peach**es**

Spelling Words

1. trips
2. buses
3. classes
4. eggs
5. wishes
6. boxes
7. games
8. peaches

Challenge Words

1. lunches
2. faces

My Study List

Add your own spelling words on the back. →

Name _____

 My Study List

1. _____

2. _____

3. _____

4. _____

5. _____

6. _____

7. _____

8. _____

Additional Spelling Words

1. bushes	3. benches
2. kittens	4. stones

How to Study a Word

LOOK at the word.

SAY the word.

THINK about the word.

WRITE the word.

CHECK the spelling.

174

Name _____

 My Study List

1. _____

2. _____

3. _____

4. _____

5. _____

6. _____

7. _____

8. _____

Additional Spelling Words

1. town	3. count
2. round	4. ouch

How to Study a Word

LOOK at the word.

SAY the word.

THINK about the word.

WRITE the word.

CHECK the spelling.

174

That's Incredible!: Reading-Writing Workshop

Look carefully at how these words are spelled.

Spelling Words

1. who
2. a lot
3. were
4. many
5. our
6. friend
7. cannot
8. here

Challenge Words

1. heard
2. again

My Study List

Add your own spelling words on the back.

An Octopus Is Amazing

The Vowel Sound in ball

a → **a**ll, c**a**ll

aw → s**aw**, dr**aw**

Spelling Words

1. all
2. call
3. draw
4. saw
5. small
6. ball
7. fall
8. paw

Challenge Words

1. crawl
2. also

My Study List

Add your own spelling words on the back.

Name _____

 My Study List

1. _____

2. _____

3. _____

4. _____

5. _____

6. _____

7. _____

8. _____

Additional Spelling Words

1. talk   3. claw

2. walk   4. hall

How to Study a Word

LOOK at the word.

SAY the word.

THINK about the word.

WRITE the word.

CHECK the spelling.

Name _____

 My Study List

1. _____

2. _____

3. _____

4. _____

5. _____

6. _____

7. _____

8. _____

Additional Spelling Words

1. first   3. would

2. today   4. could

How to Study a Word

LOOK at the word.

SAY the word.

THINK about the word.

WRITE the word.

CHECK the spelling.

Bringing the Rain to Kapiti Plain

Words Ending in ed or ing

clap + p + ed ⟶ clap**ped**

hug + g + ing ⟶ hug**ging**

Spelling Words

1. dropped
2. clapped
3. getting
4. stopped
5. sitting
6. stepped
7. hugging
8. shopping

Challenge Words

1. quitting
2. wrapped

My Study List

Add your own spelling words on the back. ⟶

That's Incredible!: Spelling Review

Spelling Words

1. games
2. brown
3. fall
4. wishes
5. saw
6. peaches
7. trips
8. mouse
9. paw
10. cannot
11. classes
12. many
13. house
14. friend
15. small
16. here

See the back for Challenge Words.

My Study List

Add your own spelling words on the back. ⟶

Name_____

 My Study List

1. _____
2. _____
3. _____
4. _____
5. _____
6. _____
7. _____
8. _____

Challenge Words

1. again   3. faces
2. also   4. about

How to Study a Word

LOOK at the word.

SAY the word.

THINK about the word.

WRITE the word.

CHECK the spelling.

Name_____

 My Study List

1. _____
2. _____
3. _____
4. _____
5. _____
6. _____
7. _____
8. _____

Additional Spelling Words

1. skipped   3. rubbed
2. fitting   4. begged

How to Study a Word

LOOK at the word.

SAY the word.

THINK about the word.

WRITE the word.

CHECK the spelling.

Tell Me a Tale: Reading-Writing Workshop

Look carefully at how these words are spelled.

Spelling Words

1. tried
2. never
3. going
4. coming
5. new
6. very
7. other
8. started

Challenge Words

1. enough
2. through

My Study List

Add your own spelling words on the back. ⟶

Two of Everything

The Vowel Sound in boy

oy ⟶ t**oy**, j**oy**

oi ⟶ c**oi**n, sp**oi**l

Spelling Words

1. joy
2. coin
3. oil
4. toy
5. join
6. boy
7. spoil
8. boil

Challenge Words

1. voice
2. moist

My Study List

Add your own spelling words on the back. ⟶

Name_____

 My Study List

1. _____

2. _____

3. _____

4. _____

5. _____

6. _____

7. _____

8. _____

Additional Spelling Words

1. point   **3.** foil

2. soil   **4.** joint

How to Study a Word

LOOK at the word.

SAY the word.

THINK about the word.

WRITE the word.

CHECK the spelling.

Name_____

 My Study List

1. _____

2. _____

3. _____

4. _____

5. _____

6. _____

7. _____

8. _____

Additional Spelling Words

1. something   **3.** outside

2. school   **4.** people

How to Study a Word

LOOK at the word.

SAY the word.

THINK about the word.

WRITE the word.

CHECK the spelling.

Tell Me a Tale: Spelling Review

Spelling Words

1. toy
2. shared
3. clapped
4. making
5. coin
6. shopping
7. riding
8. boil
9. other
10. boy
11. never
12. sitting
13. started
14. liked
15. new
16. stopped

See the back for Challenge Words.

My Study List

Add your own spelling words on the back. ➡

The Legend of the Indian Paintbrush

More Words Ending in
ed **or** ing
fade – e + ed ➝ fad**ed**
use – e + ing ➝ us**ing**

Spelling Words

1. making
2. used
3. faded
4. taking
5. placed
6. shared
7. riding
8. liked

Challenge Words

1. gazed
2. framed

My Study List

Add your own spelling words on the back. ➡

Name _____

 My Study List

1. _____
2. _____
3. _____
4. _____
5. _____
6. _____
7. _____
8. _____

Additional Spelling Words

1. closed   3. saving
2. hiding   4. loved

How to Study a Word

LOOK at the word.
SAY the word.
THINK about the word.
WRITE the word.
CHECK the spelling.

Name _____

 My Study List

1. _____
2. _____
3. _____
4. _____
5. _____
6. _____
7. _____
8. _____

Challenge Words

1. enough   3. voice
2. gazed   4. wrapped

How to Study a Word

LOOK at the word.
SAY the word.
THINK about the word.
WRITE the word.
CHECK the spelling.

1 A short vowel sound may be spelled **a, e, i, o,** or **u.**

hat	top
pet	fun
pin	

2 Two consonant sounds said close together may be spelled **st, tr, dr, gl, ft, sl,** or **ld.**

star	**gl**ad
just	le**ft**
trip	s**l**ip
drove	ol**d**

3 The sound that begins **show** may be spelled **sh,** and the sound that ends **much** may be spelled **ch.**

she	**ch**in
wi**sh**	mu**ch**

4 The sound that begins **when** may be spelled **wh.** The sounds that begin **thin** and **that** are both spelled **th.**

what	wi**th**
there	

5 The long **a** sound may be spelled **ai, ay,** or **a**-consonant-**e.**

tr**ai**n	m**a**d**e**
pl**ay**	g**a**m**e**

6 The long **e** sound may be spelled **ee, ea,** or **e**-consonant-**e.**

t**ea**m	n**ee**d
r**ea**d	th**e**s**e**

7 The long **o** sound may be spelled **oa, ow,** or **o**-consonant-**e.**

c**oa**t	h**o**m**e**
sl**ow**	

8 The long **i** sound may be spelled **i**-consonant-**e**.

size   like

9 The long **u** sound may be spelled **u**-consonant-**e**.

use   cute

10 Words that end with **nd** have both the **n** and **d** sounds.

sa**nd**   a**nd**

11 In words that end with **ng** or **nk**, you may not hear the **n** sound.

thi**ng**   ho**nk**

12 In **contractions**, an apostrophe takes the place of a missing letter or letters.

you're   we'll
it's   don't

13 Add **s** to most words to mean more than one. When a word ends with **s, x, sh,** or **ch,** add **es** to name more than one.

coats   wi**shes**
bu**ses**   pea**ches**
bo**xes**

14 The final **e** in some words is dropped before adding **ed** or **ing**.

shar**ed**   tak**ing**

15 The final consonant in some words is doubled before adding **ed** or **ing**.

stop**ped**   hug**ging**

16 The vowel sound in **ball** may be spelled **aw** or **a** before **ll.**

saw   call

17 The vowel sound in **boy** may be spelled **oi** or **oy**.

oil   **joy**

18 The vowel sound in **cow** may be spelled **ow** or **ou**.

do**w**n   m**ou**se

19 The vowel + **r** sounds may be spelled **ar, or, ore,** or **er**.

arm   st**ore**
b**or**n   ov**er**

20 The vowel sound in **moon** may be spelled **oo**.

r**oo**m   s**oo**n

21 The vowel sound in **book** may be spelled **oo**.

f**oo**t   l**oo**k

GRAMMAR GUIDE

Grammar, Capitalization, and Punctuation

SENTENCES

A **sentence** tells what someone or something did.

> We ate dinner.   The boy rode the bus.

Kinds of Sentences

A **telling sentence** tells something. It begins with a capital letter. It ends with a period.

> The horse won the race.   Cathy went to the store.

A **question** asks something. It begins with a capital letter. It ends with a question mark.

> Are you hungry?   Do you like to play soccer?

An **exclamation** shows strong feeling. It begins with a capital letter. It ends with an exclamation point.

> I loved that book!   What a fun day that was!

Naming Parts and Action Parts

Every sentence has a **naming part** and an **action part.**

The **naming part** of a sentence tells who or what.

> **Jennifer** played in the snow.   **The sky** looks beautiful today.

The **action part** of a sentence tells what is happening.

> The train **moves fast.**   Alex **laughs.**

NOUNS

A **noun** names a person, a place, or a thing.

> The **girl** likes to run.   We saw the **pig**.
>
> Shelley went to the **park**.

Special Nouns

Some nouns name special people, places, or things.

These **special nouns** begin with capital letters.

Nouns	Special Nouns
My **dog** loves to play.	**Fluffy** loves to play.
The **park** is her favorite place.	**Jefferson Park** is her favorite place.

Nouns for One and More Than One

A noun can name one person, place, or thing.

> Tommy picked up the **cat**.   She walked by the **tree**.

A noun can also name more than one person, place, or thing.

> Tommy picked up the **cats**.   She walked by the **trees**.

Add **s** to most nouns to name more than one.

> The rug**s** were wet.   The hat**s** were silly.

Add **es** to nouns that end with **s, x, ch,** and **sh**
to name more than one.

> These glass**es** are old.   The watch**es** need to be fixed.
>
> The fox**es** were playing.   The dish**es** are dry.

A few nouns change their spelling to name more than one.

> one child → two child**ren**   one man → two m**e**n
>
> one foot → two f**ee**t   one woman → two wom**e**n

PRONOUNS

A **pronoun** can take the place of a noun.

He, she, it, and **they** are pronouns.

> **Karen** likes to swim.   **She** likes to swim.
>
> **Brett** likes to swim too.   **He** likes to swim too.
>
> **Maria and Brett** meet Karen   **They** meet Karen at the pool.
> at the pool.
>
> **The water** is very warm.   **It** is very warm.

VERBS

A **verb** names an action.

> Mary **plays** the piano beautifully.
>
> The birds **fly** over the trees.
>
> The baby **drinks** the juice.
>
> I **get** my lunch.

Verbs That Tell About Now

A verb can tell about an action that is happening now.

Add **s** to a verb that tells about one.

> The cat **plays** with the ball.　　Tricia **smiles**.

Do not add **s** to a verb that tells about more than one.

> The boys **sing** songs.

Verbs That Tell About the Past

A verb can name actions that happened before now, or in the past.

Add **ed** to a verb to show that something happened in the past.

> We **walked** to the store.
>
> Marta **called** her on the phone.
>
> Kim **rowed** the boat to safety.

GRAMMAR GUIDE

Is, Are, Was, Were

Is and **are** tell about something that is happening **now**.

Use **is** with one. Use **are** with more than one.

Mr. Roberts **is** my teacher.   They **are** at home.

Was and **were** tell about something that happened in the past.

I **was** at the party yesterday.   My friends **were** already there.

Irregular Verbs

Some special verbs change spelling to tell about the past.

Have and Do

William **has** fun at the fair.   He **does** like hats.

People **have** fun at the fair.   They **do** like hats.

They **had** fun at the fair.   She **did** like hats.

Take and Make

He **takes** some cookies.   He **makes** toys.

They **take** some cookies.   The girls **make** toys.

We **took** some cookies.   Everyone **made** toys.

Throw and Break

Jimmy **throws** the ball.   The man **breaks** the glass.

The players **throw** the ball.   The workers **break** the glass.

Kara **threw** the ball.   The dog **broke** the glass.

ADJECTIVES

An **adjective** is a word that tells how something looks, feels, tastes, smells, and sounds.

The **pretty** sunset made them happy. (looks)

The child was sleeping in a **soft** blanket. (feels)

The pizza was **spicy**. (tastes)

Many flowers have a **sweet** smell. (smells)

The **loud** siren scared her. (sounds)

Adjectives can also tell size, shape, color, and how many.

The **large** cloud moved slowly.   (size)

The child had a **round** face.   (shape)

The **blue** hat is in the box. (color)

Two workers walked into the building. (how many)

Comparing with Adjectives

Add **er** to adjectives to compare two people, places, or things.

Lupe had **shorter** hair than Kelly.

Add **est** to compare more than two people, places, or things.

Lee had the **shortest** hair in the class.

CAPITALIZATION

Every sentence begins with a capital letter.

The weather is sunny.

The names of the days of the week begin with capital letters.

The party is on **T**uesday.

The names of months begin with capital letters.

We go camping every year in **A**ugust.

The names of holidays begin with capital letters.

I want to buy my mother a **M**other's **D**ay gift.

A title begins with a capital letter.

Put a period after **Mrs., Mr., Ms.,** and **Dr.**

The title **Miss** does not have a period.

Mrs. Jackson	**Ms.** Sloane	**Dr.** Lee
Mr. Fernandez	**Miss** Jones	

The first word, the last word, and each important word in a book title begin with a capital letter. Book titles are underlined.

I like the book **B**ringing the **R**ain to **K**apiti **P**lain.

PUNCTUATION

Ending Sentences

A telling sentence ends with a period.

All of Timmy's friends will be at the party.

A question ends with a question mark.

Will there be balloons and cake at the party?

An exclamation ends with an exclamation point.

That cake was really good!

Contractions

Use an apostrophe in contractions to take the place of missing letters.

isn't (is not)	it's (it is)
can't (cannot)	I'm (I am)
wouldn't (would not)	they've (they have)
wasn't (was not)	they'll (they will)
we're (we are)	you're (you are)

Comma

Use a comma between the day and the year in dates.

My sister was born August 22, 1995.

Use a comma between the name of a city and the name of a state.

We went on a trip to Phoenix, Arizona.

Her family lives in San Jose, California.

PROOFREADING CHECKLIST

Read each question. Check your paper for each kind of mistake.
Correct any mistakes you find.

- ☐ Did I begin each sentence with a capital letter?
- ☐ Did I use the correct end mark?
- ☐ Did I spell each word correctly?
- ☐ Did I indent each paragraph?

PROOFREADING MARKS

Mark	Meaning	Example
∧	Add one or more words.	I ∧ see the play. *(want to)*
—	Take out one or more words.	The boat ~~did~~ moved slowly.
	Change the spelling.	The cloud ~~filed~~ the sky. *(filled)*
/	Make a capital letter a small letter.	The A̸nimals hid from the storm.
☰	Make a small letter a capital letter.	There are thirty days in april.

| TOO MANY TAMALES | NOW ONE FOOT, NOW THE OTHER | A CHAIR FOR MY MOTHER | CLEAN YOUR ROOM, HARVEY MOON! |
High-Frequency Words	High-Frequency Words	High-Frequency Words	High-Frequency Words
laugh	carried	brought	clean
?	?	?	?
light	mean	buy	done
?	?	?	?
nearly	picture	fall	few
?	?	?	?
second	warm	four	notice
?	?	?	?
white	word	full	should
?	?	?	?
	year	world	shout
?	?	?	?
			today
?	?	?	?
?	?	?	?
?	?	?	?
?	?	?	?

CLEAN YOUR ROOM, HARVEY MOON! Spelling Words	A CHAIR FOR MY MOTHER Spelling Words	NOW ONE FOOT, NOW THE OTHER Spelling Words	TOO MANY TAMALES Spelling Words
room	jar	for	better
?	?	?	?
moon	arm	more	after
?	?	?	?
book	hard	or	over
?	?	?	?
soon	are	story	under
?	?	?	?
look	start	born	mother
?	?	?	?
noon	car	short	father
?	?	?	?
broom	far	store	sister
?	?	?	?
foot	dark	corn	brother
?	?	?	?
cookie	apart	before	counter
?	?	?	?
cartoon	charcoal	morning	center
?	?	?	?

AN OCTOPUS IS AMAZING	WHAT HAPPENED TO PATRICK'S DINOSAURS?	THE DAY JIMMY'S BOA ATE THE WASH
High-Frequency Words	High-Frequency Words	High-Frequency Words
also	cold	class
?	?	?
between	guess	egg
?	?	?
draw	later	farm
?	?	?
eight	leave	finally
?	?	?
seven	often	hurry
?	?	?
		sound
?	?	?
?	?	?
?	?	?
?	?	?
?	?	?

THE DAY JIMMY'S BOA ATE THE WASH	WHAT HAPPENED TO PATRICK'S DINOSAURS?	AN OCTOPUS IS AMAZING
Spelling Words	Spelling Words	Spelling Words
trips	how	all
?	?	?
buses	out	call
?	?	?
classes	now	draw
?	?	?
eggs	house	saw
?	?	?
wishes	down	small
?	?	?
boxes	brown	ball
?	?	?
games	cow	fall
?	?	?
peaches	mouse	paw
?	?	?
lunches	about	crawl
?	?	?
faces	shower	swallow
?	?	?

| THE LEGEND OF THE INDIAN PAINTBRUSH | TWO OF EVERYTHING | BRINGING THE RAIN TO KAPITI PLAIN |
High-Frequency Words	High-Frequency Words	High-Frequency Words
ago	enough	change
?	?	?
different	excited	cloud
?	?	?
earth	person	happen
?	?	?
shall	poor	heavy
?	?	?
slowly	pull	rain
?	?	?
those	quickly	stood
?	?	?
		wild
?	?	?
?	?	?
?	?	?
?	?	?

BRINGING THE RAIN TO KAPITI PLAIN	TWO OF EVERYTHING	THE LEGEND OF THE INDIAN PAINTBRUSH
Spelling Words	Spelling Words	Spelling Words
dropped	joy	making
?	?	?
clapped	coin	used
?	?	?
getting	oil	faded
?	?	?
stopped	toy	taking
?	?	?
sitting	join	placed
?	?	?
stepped	boy	shared
?	?	?
hugging	spoil	riding
?	?	?
shopping	boil	liked
?	?	?
quitting	voice	gazed
?	?	?
wrapped	moist	framed

second	full	clean
white	world	done
class	carried	few
egg	mean	notice
farm	picture	should
finally	warm	shout
hurry	word	today
sound	year	brought
cold	laugh	buy
guess	light	fall
later	nearly	four

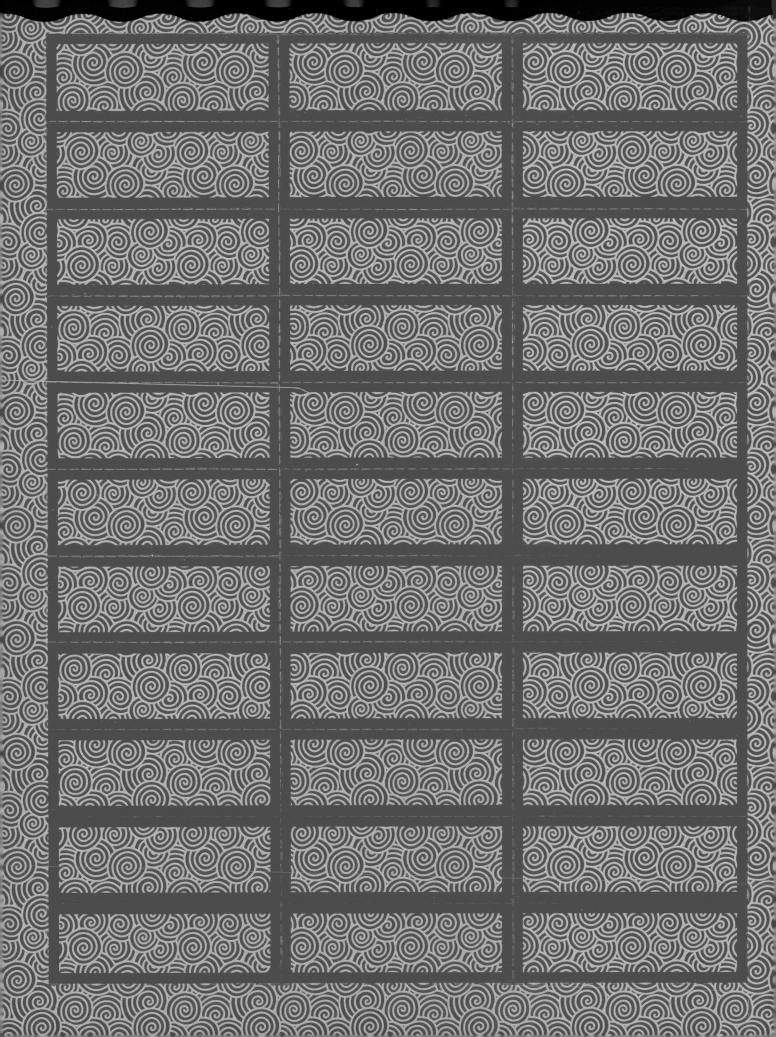